Through the Eyes
of My Soul

A Journey of Faith

Morella Echenagucia-Carta

"It is not how much we give, but how much love we put into given"

St. Mother Theresa of Calcutta

To my grandchildren Vicky, Petey, Finn and future ones, who inspired me to write this book.
To my sons Nelson Marcel, Odoardo Jose and Eduardo Jose, who gave me the gift of becoming a mom!

Acknowledgments

I want to thank,

- Dr. Solomon Kabuka for giving me the idea to write the book and for his priceless job editing my original manuscripts.

-Father Francis Nwakile, for his guidance as I wrote the chapter about my Faith.

-My niece Andreina Navarro for designing the logo of our organization in Uganda.

-Jean Kaye for showing me the gift of servicing others in Uganda, and for her friendship and guidance.

-All the donors who have trusted us to work on their behalf saving children lives in Uganda.

-Special thanks to my anonymous friend, whose generosity has been a cornerstone of every fundraising campaign.

-Father Bernard Kirlin, whose guidance supported my spiritual growth.

-Alvareze, our family writer for his foreword.

-Elisa Arraiz, whose professional guidance was key to finalize this book.

-Alfredo Sainz for a beautiful design of the book cover.

I also want to thank many people who came to my life supporting me with love and patience since the beginning of my journey.

CONTENT

FOREWORD

I can perfectly remember the day I decided that Batman was going to be my hero or more precisely, an idol, someone to look up to. I remember coming to that conclusion based on the human side of a superhero, with no superpowers whatsoever.

It was fun, it was nice imagining that I could be as cool as someone like Batman. Those days were gone quickly as the Teenage Mutant Ninja Turtle came along. However, these days went fast too. Meanwhile, I was finding who I wanted to be on the mystery pages of Sherlock Holmes's cases.

After many superheroes and fictional characters, the teen years hit me with more human-like heroes. Mother Theresa, Pope John Paul II, Nelson Mandela, and many others started to catch my attention and with them, more attainable dreams. The idea of becoming someone as good and flawed as any of us gave me reasons to fall in love with the idea of becoming someone who impacts the world. My dreams evolved into a more realistic view of the world. It was fun as well, and it was a challenge.

As the Argentine cartoonist, Quino, once said "life and reality are like a swing, the fun ends as soon as you put your feet on the ground." The sooner you realize that you can't be anyone else but yourself, the better. It took me a long time to understand.

Once you hit the world you set up to impact, reality comes in like a hammer. It teaches us important lessons we avoid accepting. Excuses are handy when we try to explain this thing called adulthood. Moreover, how was I going to be like Mandela if I wasn't even borne in South Africa? Also, it was too late for me to become a priest or a nun.

For some of us, the challenges of just being ourselves could cause a serious case of "life on autopilot". The only way to awaken is when something out of the ordinary, or in my case something quite ordinary, makes you snap.

That moment for me was when I realized my real heroes and idols were living next to me all my life. I had the luck to find them right there within my large family, and of course, among them my dear auntie Moe. I remember when my mom told me about my aunt going to live in New York because some fancy bank was "stealing" her away from us. I remember spending a month in her Darien-Connecticut wonderful and cozy home. Watching her walk at full speed, after getting down on Grand Central Station. She talked to me about real diversity in a big city like New York. I thought New York was big but after that trip to Moe's house, I realized New York was bigger than I expected. I learned that I didn't need to impact the entire world, just the one around me. I realized I should do it as my aunt, my idol, and the real heroes of the world were doing on every corner.

Nowadays I walk my path with the safety net of what I've learned from regular and extraordinary people like my aunt Morella Echenagucia-Carta.

In her book, she describes in a simple and honest way each of the phases of her growth in faith. Most of all, how the call to put her faith into action caused her to leave the comfort that surrounds her for the work of serving abused and abused children in Uganda. This is why I realized that my real heroes and idols were living next to me all my life.

I'm dying to talk to you about all the things you will learn after finishing this book, but I know you deserve to discover Moe's life, not exactly how I did it, but through her own eyes.

Dalvareze
Author of "The Verbedines, La Leyenda del Arcano"

Prologue

I never thought about writing a book. I thought authors must be excellent writers, experienced novelists, philosophers, or scientists, offering topics attractive enough to future readers.

One day, while I was in our Transition Home in Uganda, I woke up thinking that if something happened to me, my grandchildren were going to miss part of my story, my intimate story told directly by me; the story through my own eyes.

Unfortunately, in the world we are living, my grandchildren live three hours by plane far from me; some in Venezuela and others in New York/ New Jersey. With the limitations of frequent interactions, I had two options. The first one was to expect my sons to pass some aspects of my life to their children, risking misinterpretations; and the second, to tell them directly through the eyes of my soul about the person I was. I decided on option two; I opened my laptop and immediately started to type.

As I was writing, it was fascinating to realize how every part of my story was concatenated. The realization of how even the not-so-happy days, had a purpose in my life was amazing. I didn't comprehend the experiences as they were happening to me. As time has passed, I realized they all had a meaning, they all made sense.

I described how my faith grew from being raised in a comfortable life, to a life devoted to protecting the lives and the healthy development of abandoned and abused children in Uganda (36 hours door-to-door trip from home).

This is a story of love, failure, and success, and how all of these came together to strengthen my faith and devotion to serve others.

I am not a writer, a novelist, a philosopher or a scientist; however, I decided to let my soul speak for me. This is what made it so easy to write this book because what is written here came directly from my soul.

My objective was clear, I wanted my grandchildren to know about me and my relationship with our Lord. I wanted them to know that each life is different. There is not a one-size-fits-all, but with our eyes on the Lord, they and I will have more similarities than differences. I wanted them to know that it is ok to fail. Failure does not define who we are. It is our response to failure and determination to succeed that will. I wanted them to know that "it is not how much you give but how much love you put into given."

I hope one day, when they are old enough, they will read this book and will get to know their "Mimi" better.

Morella Echenagucia-Carta

Journey into the unknown

The desire to volunteer has been constantly with me. It was always my aspiration to do it upon retiring. Well, retiring looked very far away when I was in my 40's and 50's.

Even before I retired, I went twice to Peru in Latin America in 2012 and 2013 with a medical mission. The doctors, nurses, and volunteers in the group were, in general, very committed and spiritual. They always praised the Lord for the opportunity to serve others with love and compassion.

Before the first trip, we gathered together at the home of Dr. Reis and his wife Aida Chaparro in El Doral, Miami. We were about ten including other doctors, nurses, and volunteers in general. The purpose of the meeting was to go over the details of the trip, assign responsibilities, etc.

It was there where I met Braulio Ortiz and his wife, who have become two of my dearest friends. Trips like that one take lots of preparation, logistics, and the like. They included nurses traveling from Canada, volunteers from Florida and other states, and local volunteers from Peru.

We were asked to place our personal belongings in our carry-on bags. At Miami International Airport in Miami, we were each given two suitcases to check-in. We knew that these suitcases contained medical items and donations to distribute in Peru.

We arrived at a convent in Lima, late in the evening. We were full anticipation and excitement about the following day. At breakfast, more information was distributed, and off we left to the school where we were going to set the clinic.

The place was on the outskirts of Lima. It was in a very poor area, on a little hill. There was desert-like dust everywhere and scorching high temperature. The organizers had brought a full pharmacy, OBG doctors, pediatricians, dentists, general doctors, nurses, psychologies, and even a playroom to entertain children while their parents were busy with doctors. I was amazed by the organization and logistics to have the clinic ready on the opening day.

When the patients arrived, they went from the admission to the triage, and then they were sent to whatever specialty they needed. At the end of the process they received the medications. From there they headed to the donations room.

Two other volunteers and I were responsible for organizing the donations. The room was jammed up with boxes of donations. We could hardly move around the room. In addition to the donations we brought from the USA, we had received items from the local people to give away. We spent the first three hours organizing the clothes by age, size, and type. When we opened the doors of the room, the patients gladly looked at what they needed. We controlled the process, while helping them with their searches.

I will never forget a little girl six or seven years old. I asked her what she was looking for and she said she wanted a dress. I found a nice dress for her, a really beautiful one.

When I gave it to her, she asked me if she could keep it. When I said this is yours, she turned her face to her mother with her eyes open, full of emotions and said it was her first dress, ever. It was so easy to make a child happy with just a little effort. There were so many other cases like this one; even adults were extremely grateful for what we gave them. If we all knew how little effort is needed to make a child or an adult happy, if we all knew the feeling of showing love and appreciation to those in need, if only we all understood that an act of love is what Jesus is asking us to do, what a world we would have!

At the end of each day, back at the convent, we had a debriefing about what we had experienced and its impact on our lives. We registered what we had learned during the day.

The clinic lasted three days, from Friday to Sunday. During this period, we received over 3000 patients. They all left with deep gratitude for the service and donations received.

The second year in Peru was even more rewarding to me. I worked with the pediatrician, Dr. Aida Chaparro, as her assistant. She taught me patience, love, and compassion with every child we saw.

The majority of the young patients were almost deaf until the doctor looked at their ears and cleaned them up; we found objects ranging from clay, clips, beans, etc. The surprise expressed in their faces after getting their ears cleaned was unbelievable. They could clearly hear!

The little babies were always nervous and crying. I found myself especially drawn to caring and calming them down. I really enjoyed serving those kids. My desire to help others was getting focused on this age group, zero to six years!

During these two medical missionary trips, I met a young American, thirty-something. He was living in Peru. He had decided to stay there for several years to help those in need. It was difficult for me to understand how a young professional would leave the American comfort, move to an impoverished place in Peru to live and serve others. There were several others in the group who were like him. I questioned myself, would I ever be able to do that? Would I be able to leave behind the comfort I had back in USA and be focused on helping others? I didn't answer but the question was always in my mind...

At the end of the last trip, my friend Luisa Pantin, Braulio, and his wife Hilda decided to continue on to Machu Picchu. We flew from Lima to Cusco and spent a few days visiting several beautiful towns around Cusco and the Sacred Valley. On the day of the trip to Machu Picchu, our emotions and expectations were very high. However, nothing prepared us for what we were going to see and feel. The serenity and energy of the place were amazing. More questions than answers came to our minds. How was it possible that those people in the 15th century, moved those rocks of about one ton each from a very distant place to the Inca citadel situated on a mountain ridge 2,430 meters above sea level? Definitely, a highly advanced civilization by far! What happened to them? Where are they now?

Luisa and I went all the way to the top of the mountain while Braulio and Hilda waited for us halfway to the top. I will never forget the feeling of peace I felt there. I think a better word is "serenity". It was a great trip that strengthened our friendship, for sure!

After Peru, I went back to my daily routine of working from home in Miami while attending to my sick husband. Sometimes I went back and forth from Miami to New York where my office was located.

After my husband passing in 2014, I worked for another year, and then I decided to retire. I had a burning desire to help others. I did some local research and applied for volunteering opportunities in a variety of local organizations in Miami. Some worked well and some were not what I was looking for. There was one in particular that I wish I had continued. I did it for four years. I used to bring the Holy Communion to the sick at Mount Sinai Medical Center in Miami Beach.

In order to obtain my id as part of the volunteer group and be able to visit patients, I was given an orientation to every area of the hospital. In addition, I had to take basic immunizations to protect patients and be protected from getting sick.

Talking to patients, sharing my faith without being pushing, praying with them, or just listening to their concerns and stories; sometimes even hugging them when they were sad, all made me feel I was born to serve others. With every patient I visited I learned something new. Above all I learned to thank God for my health and the family He gave me.

There were many patients who were very lonely, sad, and left there with no family visitors. One of the patients had been in a coma for four years. His family never visited him because if they showed up, the hospital was going to request a payment. By not having a family to take responsibility, the poor man was left at the hospital care for four years until he finally died. Very sad story!

One day I visited a stage 4 Cancer patient I will call Sharon. She was always complaining about everything and was very bitter about life in general. She didn't allow anybody inside her room, let alone get closer to her. According to her everybody was full of germs. One day, she permitted my access to her room and we started chatting about her beliefs and mine. She said she believed in

God but didn't want to know anything about priests, Confession, or Communion. Every Wednesday when she saw me in the hallway, she would call me and asked me to sit down next to her, but not too close as she thought I could have germs.

Many Wednesdays I spent 30 mins to an hour chatting with her. I saw her at least three consecutive months before she passed away. One day, she said she wanted to talk to a priest. I was beside myself. I run outside, called the parish, and asked for a priest. I thought, 'wow look what I have done!' It turned out that when the priest went to see her, she rushed him out. To me, this was one of the biggest lessons I learned. I have been so foolish thinking I could have convinced her to see a priest when in reality it's the Holy Spirit and only Him who could have opened her heart and convince her to repent, not me. I was only going to be a conduit. This case taught me to be humble and not to look for recognition.

Sharon passed away in room 609 of the main hospital. Every time I passed by this room, I remember her and pray for her soul, knowing our Lord in His infinite mercy took care of her.

I also volunteered for an organization called Mater Filius or Mother and Child in Latin. This is an organization that protects pregnant women, who have been left alone by their families and partners because of the pregnancy.

I was attracted to Mater Filius after I saw a video of the founder Miriam Vasquez from Mexico. She described about her encounter with Virgin Mary, who asked her to protect the life of the unborn. The message really touched me! I did some research and found out that there was a group already working to open a Mater Filius home in Florida. I joined the group in 2016. In 2017, I traveled with part of the group to Mexico for their global convention. The mission was spreading very fast to several cities in Mexico, the USA, and Latin America. It was there where I met Miriam and her husband Jose Manuel. They both inspire peace, action, love, and compassion. I worked with them for about two years. Up to this day we have remained good friends. They have found a house in Miami area. Hopefully soon they will start supporting needy pregnant girls and help them care for their babies. A beautiful mission indeed.

I also became very engaged with the parish I go to, St Mary Magdalen in Sunny Isle Beach. I still work in the parish administration as well as serving in the altar as a lector and as an extraordinary minister of the Holy Communion. The former pastor, Father Bernard Kirlin enhanced my faith by his numerous teaching and constant reminder of the Lord's mercies. With him, I had one of the best confessions I ever had. I felt like I downloaded all my concerns, fears, as well as my successes and failures in life. He just listened, never judgmental. He accompanied me in my spiritual journey and kept reminding me of the love of our Lord. He emphasized to me that the Lord has a short memory when we sincerely repent; that there is no need to keep torturing ourselves for sins that have been confessed because those sins have been forgiven. I said, "what if I have forgotten a specific sin and didn't confess it?" He said that when we receive the absolution, the priest says all your sins have been forgiven! I have so much to thank him! He is now retired but I pray for him every day.

I continued with my search for volunteering opportunities. The jobs I had in Corporate America were for the most part international. I missed dealing with different cultures in different countries. Therefore, I decided to search for volunteer opportunities abroad. I wanted something in Central America to use my Spanish. However, the first overseas opportunity that opened up for me was to Malawi. After I thought about it, I applied, and in a month, I was on my way to Africa with a medical mission.

The Malawi group consisted of three doctors, about 12 nurses, one lady like me coming from the banking industry with no medical background, as well as the organizer, Jean Kaye from HELP International.

Our connection in Washington-DC was delayed. When we arrived in Addis Ababa, Ethiopia, the flight to Malawi had departed. We stayed at a modest hotel and had dinner before venturing out to see some local dancers.

At the hotel, after dinner, the restaurant hosts asked us to sit on the floor. They started to roast the coffee while they served popcorn on plates but also spread popcorn around us on the floor. When the coffee was ready, they served it and we started to enjoy popcorn. We later understood that they do this every night with their families as a time to share their highs and lows during the day, as opposed to our culture where we have our cellphone or television on all the time.

Immediately after, we went to see the local dancers. Mostly, dancers moved their shoulders more than their hips while they made a deep sound. Drums let out their typical noises as they responded to the beats of local skillful drummers. It was a great opportunity to experience Ethiopian culture. The entire evening vividly brought to life my Western images of Africa. Finally, I was in Africa!

The following day, we continued our journey to Malawi. We arrived at Lilongwe, the country's capital. Malawi, a landlocked country is in the south-east of Africa, with a population of about eighteen million people. It is surrounded by Tanzania, Zambia, and Mozambique. It is extremely poor but with pleasant people and whose children's eyes depict a sense of happiness.

Around five in the evening, we arrived at the compound owned and run by David Cufaro and his wife. David is an American retiree who, with his wife founded the Healing Hope Church. They also built an elementary school and later a high school. All these establishments are part of their compound. It also houses some 10,000 chickens, garden of vegetables, etc. David was also very focused on spreading the word of God to remote areas in Malawi. He is a devout Christian.

Upon arrival, we were met by the residents of the village. They greeted us with joy and excitement, singing beautiful songs from their hearts. They all knew the songs, and they sounded like angels singing with one voice.

We were all touched by the reception we got. The fact that their songs came directly from their hearts made an instant impact on all of us. We were holding up our tears.

The following day, our first clinic was at the same compound. We saw adults and children. They were suffering mainly from Malaria, malnutrition, and body pain. The body pains were the results of working in the fields or carrying water on top of their heads, from the wells to their houses. There was no running water in their homes.

One day, we packed medicines, benches for patients to sit, plus everything needed to set up a one-day clinic in a very remote location. It was almost two hours from the compound. We traveled in a truck similar to the one used by the military, open in the rear with only a bench on each side. An uneven road was full of dust which found its way into our hair and gave us a new reddish hair coloring. Throughout the entire journey the uneven road made us jump up and down from our seats like sacks of beans. Male travelers in the group marveled at how females held tight with our boobs forcefully bouncing on our chests.

We travelled through an area that was almost deserted. We saw small shacks distantly separated; encountered people walking in the middle of the road, carrying water or food on their heads, and babies wrapped around the backs of their mothers. As we passed people, we were very happy to see children chanting out loud the local word for "whites." Children were children, and as they saw our truck they tried to run after us with their little voices trying to catch our attention. When we waved back, they got excited as if they were in heaven!

When we finally arrived at the predetermined place, there were about two thousand people waiting to see a doctor. Many of them traveled by foot from remote areas 20-30 kilometers away, with no water; and some of them without shoes and with several children in their hands. However, they were chanting and happy to see us. We were very nervous because of the number of people waiting under a very hot sunny day and no water. They had been waiting for a few hours and were so exhausted that many were sleeping on the muddy and dusty ground.

As a precaution, Jean our group leader told us that in case people became agitated, she or any one of us would blow a whistle. At the sound of the whistle we all were directed to leave everything behind and run to the truck. Thank God, Jean was able to organize and control the mob. There was no agitation. Quite the opposite, the people were all very patient and happy to see a doctor.

I was doing the easy part, taking the vitals. I kept admiring the patients. I saw people sleeping on the floor tired after the long journey. Yet, they still had to go back to their homes the same way they had come, on foot! As for me, after a few hours of bending while taking their vitals, my lower back had started to hurt. Sara, the other volunteer like me, had the assignment of taking care of all the members of our team. She constantly reminded us to drink water and to relax a few minutes, from time to time. When she saw my tired face, she gave me a tiger balm lotion to rub my back. I was tired and hot because the temperature must have been in the 40 degrees Celsius, over 100 degrees Fahrenheit. The tiger balm made my pain go away for a few minutes but then it came back, over and over, stronger and stronger.

One of the patients was a humble man in his 80ths. He was very thin, wore no shoes, a jacket torn in threads and a decaying long sleeves shirt that he displayed with pride. I will never forget what happened to me when I helped him to remove his jacket and roll up his sleeves. When I touched his all-bone arm, I felt like I was touching Jesus's arms. I wanted to hug him and say so many things to him. Even with the language barrier, I think we both understood the special time we shared. Our eyes crossed and without any word between us, we said everything. We shared that moment intensively. I don't know what he felt but I know he also felt something special because his eyes said everything. I have thought many times about this incident. Through much of my life, I believe God had sent me a message about what He wanted me to do. That message was and still is to help and love those in need. The burning sensation in my heart was growing by the minute!

I can only say that after the incident with the old man, all my back pain either disappeared or I just was so emotionally touched that it didn't bother me anymore. I continued doing what I was doing, treating each person with love and care. We didn't understand each other's words. In Africa, there are many languages and limited English knowledge. However, for me it was very easy. We communicated with our hearts. My heart was burning with the desire to hug each patient as I started to see Jesus' face in each pair of eyes. I think this experience marked a major transformation in my life. From henceforth I tend to see every person, through their eyes, as if I have Jesus in-front of me.

Every night at the mission, right after dinner, our group would sit together for a debriefing about the day's highs and lows. Immediately the debriefing, the children of the families living in the compound, would come and sing songs, and play with us. There was one child in particular who caught our attention because at the age of five, she knew several psalms word by word.

After two missions to Malawi, I seriously considered staying in Malawi. However, in retrospect, I think I was afraid or just not ready yet to start as a missionary.

As a group, being so far away from our homes and going through many emotional situations, we developed a strong bond as missionaries. To this day, we are in touch through social media. Some of us have traveled together on subsequent missions to Africa.

At the end of our first mission, we traveled five to six hours someplace in northern Malawi to visit a national animal park . In reality, it was our time to decompress from our high charged emotions generated by our missionary experience. We all enjoyed the safari very much. It was my first safari ever.

While in Malawi, I was deeply troubled by seeing children without shoes walking on hot surfaces. When I returned to the USA, I contacted a manufacturing company in China and bought 3000 pairs of shoes for children and adults. I had the order sent directly to Malawi. Six months later, six of us from the first trip returned to Malawi to distribute those shoes.

Seeing the faces of adults and children when they were trying on the shoes was the best payback for me. We made them happy for one day or as long as those shoes lasted; or perhaps forever! We were on the floor, trying to find the right size for each kid but first, we had to remove the dirt and mud from their feet. We also gave them some toys I brought from my trip to Peru. They included pencils with a little doll on top, wheel cars that Marielita my niece had donated, and many other gifts. They were very inexpensive toys but of huge value to the kids who had never received such gifts. Their faces lighted up with appreciation and joy. The six of us were holding our tears with every child we served.

There is nothing more rewarding than loving and serving others. I wish people can experience the feeling received after an act of giving. It has no comparison. We are fortunate to have received everything we have. Sharing just a little with people in need has an exponential return! Giving is an act of love and the reward is priceless; we give but we receive more in return! It is like an addiction, the more you give the more you want to give.

One day, Jean Kaye, Jenifer, and I visited the Chief of the Tribe from the area where the mission was located. A young man in his late twenties. He "inherited" the tribe from his late father when he was only 17 years old. We were surprised by his level of maturity and balance when we spoke about different topics including the education and health of his people. He showed us all the memorabilia he had about the day he was named his father's successor. At the end of the visit, in a very interesting ritual, he gave Jean a special ceremonial hat with feathers and an arrow. He named her his mother. To Jen and me he gave us long beautiful necklaces. He named us his sisters. I still have the neckless.

At the end of the second visit to Malawi, the team and I also went for a safari to decompress our emotions. In the middle of the safari, our trolly car stopped. We waited for an hour until the park authorities came to our rescue. Waiting time was spent watching monkeys and other animals from a distance, while they too watched us. We were a bit nervous. Thankfully, around seven in the evening the rescue came.

During this second trip to Malawi Jean Kaye, the CEO of HELP International, asked me if I would like to go to Uganda with her. After figuring out where in Africa was Uganda, I thought about it and said, "I'm in." I never knew at that time that Uganda was going to be the turning point in my life; a life-changing experience from all angles...

My Roots

I was lucky to be born on June 2nd, 1952, into a wonderful family of Pedro Echenagucia and Esperanza Lovera. This is the beginning of my story; a seed planted and nurtured by this amazing couple, whose love and dedication shaped my life forever.

My Family

My parents grew up in two contiguous towns, Ocumare del Tuy for my dad, and Charallave for my mom; about one hour from Caracas, the capital of Venezuela. They were only 13 and 12 years old when they placed their eyes on each other.

Every Saturday, my dad used to bike through the not very smooth road to see my mom. My dad was one of eleven siblings and my mom one of six. Having big families was the norm at that time.

My father's family was very well known in Ocumare and in Caracas where he and his brothers were the owners of the famous "Echenagucia Hermanos", importers of a variety of goods, from butter to cars. Caracas was a very small city where everybody knew everybody. My dad eventually split from his brothers and later founded with uncle Jacobo, "Guariquito" a well-known store specializing in hunting and fishing, which were my dad's favorites hobbies.

My paternal grandfather went to college but never encouraged his children to have higher education. My dad's highest level of education was middle school.

My mom, on the other hand, lost her mom when she was only three years old. My maternal grandfather had very limited resources. It was his sister in-law Armanda, who helped him in raising his children. We always refer to her as "Abuela Armanda" or grandma Armanda. My mom's highest level of education was elementary school.

They were 19 and 18 years old, when they decided to marry and start a family. At that time, they didn't have much money, but were very much in love. They spent the next 17 years having eight girls, no boys. I am lucky number seven. They lived enamored of each other until death broke them apart! One month shy of celebrating their 74th year of marriage, dad passed away, followed by mom four months later.

My parents were an endless fountain of love for me and my siblings. The two endlessly demonstrated love for each other and untiring love for the family they built. I will never forget that during my visits to Venezuela after I moved to the USA, they used to place a rolling bed in their bedroom for me to share their room. The nights of my arrival, they would cut a rose from the garden and place it over my pillow. Each morning, I would wake up to a beautiful sound of these two eighty-something years of age couple sharing a kiss, seated on the edge of their bed having their coffee while waiting for me to wake up! Love was not about saying I love you but about demonstrating it with actions! I always felt special to them and I am sure my sisters felt the same. Every time I think about this, I give thanks to the Lord for the parents I got.

My parents knew how much I loved fruits; so, on every visit to Venezuela I would find a huge basket of fruits waiting for me on the kitchen table. The only problem was that they expected me to eat all the fruits on the same night of my arrival. We always laughed about it, but I loved their demonstration of love for me.

My parents made a big effort to enroll eight daughters in a Private Catholic school, Colegio San Jose de Tarbes, run by the

French Sisters of Tarbes in France; some of the nuns were Venezuelan.

It was at this school where I studied from kindergarten to High School; the formation of my spiritual and intellectual foundation. It was there where I got my First Holy Communion and Confirmation and where the sisters reinforced what we learned at home. My classmates were the same from pre-K until I graduated from High School. We all became good friends for life.

Even to this day, the class of '69 has kept connected. Around ten of us who moved to Florida frequently share afternoons and reflect on our school experiences. My first friend ever, was Judith Ayala in kindergarten. It was at her house, when I was six years, where I had my first visit to play. Her family was very special and Alfredo her dad was fun to be with. Even though Judith still lives in Caracas and I now live in Florida and we have not seen each other face to face for years, when we connect via WhatsApp, it seems to us that the time has stood still.

While at Colegio San Jose de Tarbes Irene Alliegro and Chicho Martorano became my dearest friends and up until now, we are called "The Unbreakables" because our friendship is already over sixty years old! We studied together, went to parties together, and shared so many good times together. The three of us were usually at the top of the class. Irene was the most disciplined of us, while Chicho and I followed her strict study schedule and sometimes tried to sabotage her rules!

The best place to study was at Chicho's house because Elvira, her nanny, made the best cheese sandwich, which she usually served with "Galletas Carlton" and Coke. The three of us, always studied together until 1969 when we graduated from High School. Irene went to study Pharmacy at Universidad Central de Venezuela and Chicho and I embarked on Engineering at Universidad Católica Andres Bello. That was when our problems started because Irene was always on time and Chicho and I were always relying on Irene's discipline.

We received a great education from the nuns, but the best part was what we experienced at home. My parents did not know the difference between the economist Vilfred Pareto and the mathematician Euclid of Alexandria, but they taught us the values of the Christian family life, the importance of being there for each other and to stay united no matter what; they were obsessed by the notion of keeping the family together. Years have passed and their descendants have grown to over 100 of us; yet we are very close to each other. We celebrate each other's success, weddings, birthdays, etc. Unfortunately, we all live in different countries, but technology has facilitated the connection miracle!

By the time my dad turned sixty years old, our family was growing very concerned about his life challenging hobbies. One of them was flying. Thus, my late husband gave him the golf clubs he had at home from his time in London. The idea was to provide him with an alternate hobby; we were all concerned that at one point in the future his flying license wasn't going to be renewed. Flying his small plane was one of my dad's favorites. He started golf lessons and with daily practice he became a good golfer. In time, he became a member of a golf club and spent many days, starting at 6:15 a.m. playing non-stop for decades with his group of friends.

At the golf club, he became very well regarded but his biggest recognition came from the caddies and workers at his funeral. He used to collect money from his fellow golfers to support the needs of the caddies and workers in general. At his funeral, almost all of the workers from the club and caddies came to pay their respect. I am sure my dad would have appreciated very much to see them one by one.

One day, many years after his passing, one of the caddies approached me with a golf ball that according to him used to belong to my dad. He said to me "you should have it and not me. I have kept it all these years to remember what he did for me, he made me feel loved". Right there, I said to myself, 'Don Pedro you left a mark on people's lives.' Stories like this one are many. It was not just what he did for those people but how he made them feel, appreciated, and loved.

After my dad's passing, the club decided to sponsor an annual tournament of "Bolas Criollas" under the name of Don Pedro Echenagucia. Wow, what an honor! My dad was one of the biggest proponents of building the "Bolas Criollas" court at the club, hence the club's recognition of his devotion to improving the amenities to its members.

My dad had many stories about his hunting, fishing, or flying experiences. His grandchildren loved to hear all about them. Of course, he always exaggerated a bit to make those stories even more appealing. We all laughed because we knew the tiger was not as big, or the fish did not weight 30 kgs but maybe 10 kgs, and so on. The best part of his personality was that he could talk to an adult or a child and both would be equally enthused by his experiences. Even today, when we talk about him, we all still enjoy remembering his stories and exaggerations.

When I was working at Citi-Venezuela, I called my parents to share with them the news about my promotion to Vice-president. At Citi, this is a title that recognizes seniority but not totally in the sense of the chain of command. My parents were beside themselves thinking I was the next level down from the global President of Citibank! For my parents, the family they built and what each one of us achieved in life were like jewels of the crown.

My dad was a very handsome man, tall with tan skin and attractive greenish big eyes. Maybe this was the reason why my mom was very jealous, "mucho, mucho!"

My mom also did everything in her power to support those in need. How many times did she travel to her hometown Charallave to take care of her sisters, who were in deep need of help? How many times did I see my mom supporting people who were less fortunate than we were? I recall many times poor people knocking at the door of our home, asking for food. My mom's answer was always the same "here nobody is denied a plate of food." She made an extra effort to go above and beyond the call of duty; her eight daughters served the needy with her, because she didn't know how to drive, instead she had eight drivers at her disposal!

The entire world of my mom was limited to the eight of us. She dedicated her life to my dad and us. I never heard her saying: "I cannot do it" or "I am tired." She was the definition of a "yes I can, and I will do it." She never allowed anybody to stop her from doing what she thought she had to do. Many times, I confused her determination with stubbornness; nevertheless, I wish I had half of her energy and determination. She taught us to be resilient and to never give up for what we believe!

Mami was a beautiful woman, tall, reddish hair and gorgeous blue eyes. When we were growing up if we misbehaved in front of a guest, she gave us the look of her piercing blue eyes for us to start shaking because we knew what was coming after the guest had left! At the same time, she was sweet and caring, she did everything to make sure we were prepared for the life to come. Mami was not a person to say I love you but to demonstrate with actions how much she loved us. She was always there for us, even if we didn't ask for her support. She knew how to read the writing on the wall; no way to hide a concern or a hard situation from her, she knew each one of us more than we knew ourselves.

Doña Esperanza had a strong personality, yet she was very discreet. My brothers in-law respected her very much, and for many of them she became more than just a mother in-law.

Even though her upbringing was very hard and at the age of 14 she was already sewing several dozens of shirts per week to contribute to her family, she taught herself how to prepare a nice table or to always have fresh flowers at home and how to raise eight girls with love and strong principles. She made all of our clothes including nightgowns. Whenever one of us was expecting a child, she made the most beautiful blankets and towels and prepared the "canastilla" or basket of essentials, etc. for the baby.

The family used to have Sunday's lunch at my parents' home until it grew so large that every gathering was the size of a wedding.

Then we switched to the afternoons for cake and coffee. Mom knew that my niece Marion liked the plum cake with condensed milk or Lilian liked the "buñuelos", and so on. Mom wanted each of us to feel special. She prepared something for each person. I miss these gatherings very much.

After my dad passed away, we found out in some of his notes the following description of his life: "Esperanza and my eight daughters are like touching the moon with my fingers, this is how I feel." We were the center of the universe for our parents and they made us feel that way.

As I referenced before, I am one of eight girls. I am number seven. My sisters are Blanca, Carmen Cristina (Kico), Mariela, Yolanda, Lilian, Esperanza (Pachy), and Carolina. We all married and have three children each except Mariela, who had an overdose with five children.

My dad always added some other names to ours. For instance, Kico was Kiquito Jose Ilusion; Blanca was Blanca Sola; Mariela was Yelito; Pachy was Pachy Maria Lopez and I was Morelin Tamara. No particular reason for these additions other than to show his extra love for us. He was very proud of his eight girls, even though deep in his heart he would have liked to have a son. For instance, one of his small planes model was a Cessna-Baron. In Spanish it sounds like Varon, which refers to a male. The joke was he used to say that "My children are eight females and one male." He always said his treasures were his girls. However, we all knew that our mom was his best treasure. He would say that mom was the most beautiful woman he had ever seen.

My seven sisters and I were very close to each other when we were growing up. It was natural to be even more attached by those closer in age. Most of the sisters are two years apart. However, Pachy and I who are four years apart developed a special bond. We grew up sharing friends, vacations, and even sports. Later in our adult live we started playing golf —very bad golfers by the way.

When we were growing up, we teamed up against Carolina, the youngest. Since my mom always protected her, Pachy and I couldn't deal with it. We were probably 12 and eight and Caro only five, when we told her she was adopted. We were so bad that we said to her that there was no need for her to call my parents Mr. and Mrs. that she could continue calling them mom and dad. Obviously, Caro was constantly crying and up until now, she recalls how bad she felt by our insane attitude. What a shame! Kids!

Pachy and her husband Gustavo, like me had three boys, so it was easy for us to travel together. Our children grew up very close; also close to the rest of their cousins. My parents had all girls, but the second generation is almost full of boys and very few girls. I guess the world has to be balanced, right?

Lilian was married to William Alvarez. We all adored him as he was Yolanda's classmate and long-term friend of the family. When he passed away a year after my husband's passing, Lilian and I became even closer. We traveled together to Israel and around Florida and NYC. We have many areas in common, especially as widows. We both have found peace in our hearts. When the soul is at peace and we placed our lives in the Hands of the Lord, it is very easy for others to see it and feel it. This is how Lilian and I are today, at peace.

After my mom's passing, Blanca became the matriarch of the family; she is fun to be with and I enjoy very much being with her. Blanca has three children, five grandchildren, and four great-grandchildren. She married her cousin Raul Arocha when she was only 17 years old. They have been married for over 65 years. If someone knows the definition of resilience, it's her. She had several accidents and illnesses. However, with each setback, she picked up the pieces and started all over again. Even though she lost three fingers in an accident, she continued to paint, knit, sew, cook, etc., etc. She is the epitome of the courageous woman, as nothing has stopped her.

Unfortunately, my second sister Kico is suffering from Parkinson's disease and is now living in Chile with her children. Kico was always my mentor and my role model. When I was in my twenties I just wanted to look and talk like her; I even bought my clothes in the same place she did. She is also my Confirmation godmother and my oldest son's Baptism godmother. Kico's husband, Federico Torres passed away after a long illness. Kico and I were the closest to my dad; we used to joke with him, confided in him, and spoke to him every day.

Mariela also married her cousin Orlando. They have five children and nine grandchildren. They have been married for over fifty years. They both love nature and animals, especially goats. Many years ago, they built a bullfighting ranch, La Cruz De Hierro in Apure State, Venezuela. I am glad they no longer have it because I don't like to see bulls suffering. In 1992, we traveled with them to Seville, Spain to see the World Fair, the celebration of the Holy Week that was amazing, and spent a weeklong seeing bullfights….Ouch! The bullring is called the "Maestranza de Sevilla", very famous, beautiful place but a horrible experience. I have never been back to watch a bullfight carnage.

My sister Yoly is the one we always tease about her cooking disasters. Thank God she has a great sense of humor. She is always ready to help and support whoever needs help. She never says no, quite the opposite;

sometimes she is up to her neck but keeps saying yes, I can. She has three children and two grandchildren. She married Felix Sosa, who is a writer and used to love playing "bolas criollas" with my dad.

Carolina is my youngest sister, born after me. She married Enrique Navarro and together they have three children and three grandchildren. I will never forget the event that happened one night when our parents went out to dinner with friends. The phone rang and both Carolina and I grabbed it at the same time. We were fighting for the phone when the phone went straight to her teeth and boom, half of one front tooth broke. She didn't realize what happened but only when I started pleading for my life as I knew what my parent's reaction was going to be. She had no other option but to start laughing because, for one thing, she got me under her control.

When Carolina was about ten years, our parents added Teresita Sulbaran to our family. She was Kico's friend who gained a special place in the hearts of our parents. Thus, Teresita became sister number nine in the Echenagucia family. She is sister Kico's age, and a very spiritual and loving human being. She has been a big influence on my spiritual journey and my focus on helping those in need. Many times, I have called her asking for advice. I personally appreciate the love she dedicated to my parents. To the eight sisters, Teresita is one of us! For my children and grandchildren, Teresita is their aunt and I know that for her, we are her family and her children are our nieces and nephews.

Our family grew up very close to each other. Vacation time at home was like staying at a summer camp with friends. In Venezuela, on Christmas Day, it is little Jesus who brings the gift to the children and not Santa. My parents did everything possible to make our Christmas gifts very special. We used to place our shoes down the stairs with the letter inside and wait till Christmas day in the morning to open presents. Imagine all eight girls opening gifts at the same time, it was really fun!

We also had a very strict father, who never gave us permission for a sleepover. My sisters couldn't even attend a retreat at the school. I remember when I was in 6th grade, I was invited to a three-day retreat at the school. Since the nun knew my dad's previous strictness, she thought I was not going to obtain his permission to attend. I wanted to go so badly that I said to the nun that my father had said yes with the condition she called him directly. She did and dad feeling embarrassed had no choice but to say yes. Imagine, I was number seven and I was the first one to go to an all-girls retreat with the school nuns.

My sisters are one of the best gifts my parents left me with. I am very close to all of them. We are there for each other. We know exactly who needs help or support, or who is ill and how to comfort her. The pain of one is the pain of the other eight, the children of my sisters are also my children and vice versa. I will rather be with my sisters than with friends. The majority of the time we are together is about laughing, teasing each other, or remembering my parents' stories.

Although we are often physically apart, we are constantly in contact via WhatsApp.

My nieces and nephews are also very close among themselves. My oldest nephew Raul Alfredo is only four years younger than me. He is a medical doctor and has a heart bigger than a cathedral. He and Juli, his wife, are devoted to helping those less fortunate. I have some nieces and nephews that are really close to me and I know I will be in trouble if I mention them by name, so let me keep it like this. They know who they are!

On the other hand, I am the luckiest mother in the world. I have three sons who have given me many reasons to be thankful. Each one with his own great personality, big heart; responsible, loyal, committed to his family and very good looking! What else could I ask for?

At the time I am writing this book, I have three amazing grandchildren, Vicky, Petey and Finn. I believe they are the best gift I have ever received. I wish I lived closer to them; However, I know we have a special bond that will get even stronger as life goes on.

Grandma Armanda

When I was born, grandma was already living at our home. She never married but dedicated her life to take care of the children of her sister Blanca, that had passed away when she delivered my mom's youngest brother. For us, grandma Armanda was our real grandma. I never met my blood grandparents as they died way before my time.

Grandma was an educator in her native town, Charallave where she literally taught under a big tree. Her students adored her.

Some fifteen years after Grandma's passing, we attended the inauguration of a private primary school dedicated to her in Charallave. The owners never met her, but the local people suggested her name as someone who represented the essence of a great teacher. We were greatly surprised because we didn't know that after so many years people who never met her continue to admire her. Grandma was very humble and never mentioned all she did for others.

Grandma used to have a statue of Jesus in her bedroom and many religious memorabilia. Every night we would pray with her and she would tell us stories of Jesus and Virgin Mary. She carried this statue for years and was always adoring it with devotion.

My sisters from Yolanda down to Carolina were very close to Grandma and called her "Abuela". My oldest sisters called her aunty Armanda. She always protected the three youngest, especially Pachy, who suffered from asthma when she was very young.

I was a bit rebellious when I was 9-14 years old, even to the point of challenging one of my oldest sisters, Kico, for the control of the TV. If I started crying, grandma would come to my rescue and intervene for me to obtain the tv control!

She was the sweetest person in my life. She taught me how to pray, how to read and write, additions, multiplications, and so on. She helped me with my daily homework.

Whatever I did wrong, she hid it from the rest of the family; she spoiled me a lot!

She had a government pension because she was a public-school teacher. She used to go every month to cash out her pension at the Banco de Venezuela located in Sabana Grande, a famous street in Caracas. We all looked forward to that day because after cashing her pension she would go to a famous bakery, "Pan 900", and bring us a variety of sweets including "quesadillas" and "cachitos de jamón".

Grandma Armanda taught me how to make "suspiros" or merengues. Even to this day, I use her recipe. There isn't a day I make them that I don't remember her. I have passed the recipe to my granddaughter Vicky, who loves them. She recently told me she has enhanced the recipe!

Pachy, Carolina, and I were the closest to Grandma. She used to tell us a story with her fingers and we asked her many times to do it again and again. Recently, I found myself doing the same to my youngest grandson Finn and he loved it.

Grandma taught me to knit crochet. One day after she had passed away, I was expecting my second child and I was trying to make a little sweater for the baby, but I didn't remember how to do it. I don't know whether it was real or my imagination, but I felt her presence, and immediately my hands did the job.

I wish I can move the time back and tell her what a blessing her presence was in my life, and how much I value every teaching and moments she dedicated to me. She definitely was the first influencer on my spiritual life. She was humble, sincere, and a beautiful soul. Never looked for recognition, never asked for anything but gave us all her love and care.

One day she fell down the stairs and needed surgery at the age of 80. She said that when she was in the recovery room, one of the nurses said that "she doubted this old lady will ever walk again." Well, this was the incentive grandma needed to do everything possible to walk again, first with a walker and later with a stick. After several years, she had a heart attack and died. At that time, she had moved to her hometown and lived with her only living brother Luis Manuel and his family.

Our Vacations

When we were growing up, my parents had a small hacienda in the heart of Ocumare del Tuy, where my dad was born. The place was called "La Vega." It had a nice house, a small water tank we used to call our swimming pool, many fruit plants, a little creek we called the river, cows, chickens, few pigs, and horses.

Going to La Vega was a great adventure for all of us. Imagine my parents and eight girls! At that time, we had no cell phone, tv, or any other distraction like we have today, and yet, our time there was absolutely fabulous. We enjoyed swimming in the "large" swimming pool, milking the cows early in the morning, and walking to the orange trees with my dad to grab an orange directly from the tree, and peeling it off with dad's special knife. We all

88

looked forward to every afternoon when he was available to go looking for the best orange to eat.

Our double cousins used to live very close to La Vega in a hacienda called "El Parroyo". Uncle Bernardo was my dad's brother and aunty Berta was my mom's sister, hence our cousins were double cousins to us. The funny story was that there were seven boys and one girl. Imagine if they had been eight boys and us eight girls! We got along very well and even today we consider each other as siblings.

Going to visit them at El Parroyo was also a great adventure. We played with our cousins under a huge mango tree. We pretended that the tiny mangoes that had fallen from the tree were the cows and bulls and the tree roots that had grown above the ground were the different pastures. In addition, uncle Bernardo loved cockfights and he used to tell us stories about each one of his cocks. Some of those stories were augmented with his fantasy, which attracted our attention even though we knew some additional "ingredients" have been added to the story.

On our way to La Vega, we always stopped in Charallave, the town where my mom was born, to see aunty Soledad or Solita as she was called. When she knew we were going to see her, she made a special cheese for us we called "ombligo", a Spanish translation of bellybutton. I have no idea why we called it like that. Our visits were always a major event because we were eight girls. We always felt very much loved by both sides of our family. My parents, and especially my mom, always brought donations to some of their relatives living in that area.

At that time, going from Caracas to Ocumare was a long trip through a meandering road. The trip lasted about two-plus hours. Nowadays, there is a turnpike that reduced the trip to only 40 mins. Many times, we had to stop on the road because my sisters were feeling dizzy and needed a place to throw up. I say my sisters because I have a strong stomach and seldom felt dizzy.

By the time my dad sold La Vega, he had already a small plane. Our vacations shifted to a hacienda he built in the Apure State, called Cunavichito. It was amazing for us because it was a place to fish and tour the Cunavichito river by boat. Going fishing and catching a "pavón" was a great adventure. My dad built a small cabana that had a kitchen, bathroom, a bedroom, and open space and corridor where we hang the hammocks at night. Because this place was located in the flatlands of the country with no buildings or contamination coming from cars or manufacturers, at nights, outside the cabana, lights were no necessary as the sky was full of stars. There was not a place to point in the sky that was empty of stars. The view was something fantastic to remember.

Usually, my mom brought some food already prepared and snacks for all of us, or my dad cooked the "fish catch of the day". My mom was always complaining because when dad cooked, he left all utensils and surrounding areas of the kitchen very dirty. I love to remember their discussions because they were always funny complaining, and the following day their complaining started all over again and again, but my dad never changed!

Having a small plane was great because we visited many amazing places in Venezuela. Literally, my dad would be flying the plane and looked down to see a place large enough to land, usually, in his friend's "hatos" or haciendas. Those spaces became our dad's landing runways!

For the most part, the children of his friends were the same age as us. We were very close to Oscar and Josefina and their children Kike, Mary and Jenny Rodriguez, with whom we spent many vacations in Venezuela and abroad; likewise, Dr. Ortiz and his family and so many others my dad was a friend to.

For my parents, and specifically for my dad, every landmark in our education or our lives deserved good recognition: Either a trip to Curacao in his plane for shopping when we turned 15 years old, a trip to Florida if we finished high school, or a new car or a trip to Europe if we graduated from college. Both parents were very generous to us and very proud of our accomplishments.

Maybe because I was one of the youngest, dad wasn't too rigid with me; he often rewarded me ahead of my accomplishments. I said at the beginning of this book that I was lucky number seven!

The fact was that my dad and I had a special bond. He laughed about each one of my adventures and vice versa, enjoyed competing for who would eat more mangoes at once, or dream about what we would do if we won the lotto. This was hilarious because my mom couldn't understand our decision to do something with that money when we seldom played. We responded that it didn't matter because we both loved to dream about it.

Christmas time was the best! When we were younger everything was around Christmas Eve, because our expectations for the gifts were always high. We placed our shoes with the letters to the Holy Child on the stairs and waited until Christmas Day early in the morning to open gifts. My parents did everything possible to make this time of the year unforgettable.

Later in life, the decoration of the house was led by Kico. She determined how the tree should look, the music, the menu for the dinner, and everything in between. The rest of us followed her orders. We always made jokes about her orders, but we loved her decisions.

Immediately after the New Year, my parents had already scheduled a camping trip to the Guárico state. Unfortunately, only my oldest sisters joined them and the three youngest stayed at home with my grandma Armanda and Lilian, sister number five. She always complained that she was not older enough to go and yet, old enough to take care of her youngest sisters. The fact was that we always had fun anyway.

In 1971, students at my college went on strike, and classes were suspended. My parents had already scheduled a trip to Europe with my sister Kico and Federico her husband. Since I didn't have classes, my dad invited me to go with them (early reward before I finished college). It was my first trip to Europe, and I was very excited. We visited Paris and the south of France, Nice, Monaco, Berlin, Zurich, Geneva, and Madrid.

When we arrived in Marseille, we rented a car and traveled for a week from there to Monaco and back. We had so much fun. I suffered an overdose of chocolates! I bought a carry-on just to have boxes of chocolates all for myself. I am very glad I don't remember my weight at that time as I have a selective memory!

We visited the Hotel Negroni, one of the most exclusive hotels in the south of France; just for coffee and tea. I was only 19 years old and was very bored with the atmosphere. Every woman in her best dress, very elegant, and all of them with an educated pooch. Well, I couldn't resist, I covered my face under the table and imitated a dog bark. Immediately after, the entire restaurant became a dog symphony and the women were trying to calm down their little doggies.

My parents, sister, and Federico did not say anything until we were in the car and we all laughed non-stop.

Being in Paris for the first time was indescribable. I still remember the address of the hotel where we stayed, Victor Hugo 6-Champs-Élysées. My brother in law had studied there and was a friend of the owners. The elevator was from when God created the world, but the best part was to wake up in the morning with the smell of the croissants made by the wife of the owner, full of butter!

With Federico, I walked from the Arch of Triumph through the Champs-Élysées to the

Eiffel Tower and back to our hotel. It was a beautiful walk but a very long one. Visiting a city with someone who lives or had lived there is very interesting because as tourists we miss the day to day of the locals.

My cultural shock was to see the locals buying bread and placing them under their arms with no bag or paper to protect the bread. Even though, according to the saying, in Paris do what Parisians do, we couldn't imitate them!

Western Berlin was also a fabulous place to be. So much energy and lights in contrast to the Eastern Berlin that was so somber and opaque. When we went through the Berlin Wall, we were a bit anxious. The guards did not look friendly at all, but I got to see what humans were capable of doing to show their power against others. So sad!

We visited Zurich and Geneva, where my dad bought me my first nice watch, a Rolex. I have to clarify that at that time the Venezuelan Bolivar was very strong and for us, some expenses were very affordable. I kept the watch for years until I was robbed at home some 18 years later. We took a day trip to Chamonix and went up in a cable car to the top of the mountain where Italy, France, and Switzerland meet. From there we flew to Madrid, our last city to visit. It was so nice to arrive at a place where we shared the same language and more or less a similar culture.

After Madrid, we went back to reality and continued with classes and our daily lives.

Another trip to remember was around April 1992. My late husband and I traveled with Marianela (+) my friend and her husband

William to Lisbon and Seville. We arrived in Lisbon earlier than the check-in time, so we decided to leave the suitcases at the hotel, start touring the city, and come back later. We placed our carry-ons in the trunk of the rented car and left to the Monument to the Discoveries. This beautiful monument was built to commemorate the discovery of America.

When we came back to the car, all our belongings had been robbed! Thank God, we all had taken our passports and money with us and the rest was easily replaced. We had to go to the police to report the incident. Not a single soul spoke either Spanish or English. Since I had traveled many times to Brazil before, I was proud to tell my husband and friends that I was going to be the one talking to the police. When the police spoke to me,

I was just laughing out loud because Brazilian pronunciation of Portuguese and Portugal pronunciation are like two different languages. We didn't understand a single word! Later on, using our minds more than our words, we understood part of it.

Lisbon is a beautiful city. I felt the people were very familiar to us, since in Caracas there was a very large community of Portuguese immigrants. The flowers, the trees around the city, and neighboring areas, especially during Springtime, were very attractive.

While in Portugal, we visited Cova da Iria, in Fatima. It was there in 1917 when three children reported the apparition of our Blessed Mother Mary. They described her as "The lady more brilliant than the sun". On May 13, 1946, Pope Pius XII granted canonical coronation to the venerated image enshrined at the Chapel of the Apparitions of Fatima. On November 11, 1954, the Sanctuary of Fatima was raised to the status of a minor basilica. This visit was the best of our experience in Portugal!

From Lisbon, we flew to Seville, where the Holy Week procession, the World Exposition, and the famous bullfight fiesta were happening, all at the same time.

Spaniards mixed the solemnity of the Holy Week procession with wine and tapas along the way. At first, they were very absorbed by the Holly procession. Minutes later, they entered a bar, drank wine, ate tapas, became very loud and started laughing. Then, they turned around and went back to mourn and follow the Holly Week procession.

Since Mariela, my 3rd sister, and her husband were very much into bullfighting, we went with them to watch the fiesta. It was a beautiful atmosphere, women dressed in the typical colorful Spanish dresses with tall "peinetas" in their hair and seductive veils covering back of their heads; while the men elegantly wore ties and jackets; and yet the sweltering temperature hovered around 100 degrees! Another concern to us as tourists, the seats were so tiny and tightly squeezed close to each other that it was annoying. One of those days, there was a horrible accident when the bull rammed the matador and he died in front of us. I couldn't deal with it and decided that never in my life was I going to return to a "fiesta" like that.

Staying with my friend and her husband in Europe was a trip that I will always remember. Marianela and I were very good friends and she left us too early. I am glad we had this opportunity to enjoy our friendship.

When my children were born, we took them to different places in Venezuela. First, we went to The Angel's Fall and Canaima Park with my oldest son. When my second and third son were born, the family visited different places including Margarita Island, Disney in Orlando, and the West Coast. This last trip was during Christmas 1995, right before we moved permanently to the US. We flew to San Francisco. This city was amazing. The cable car, the views, the Fisherman's Wharf, the Lombard Street, the gorgeous Golden Gate, Ghirardelli Square, and much more, were all awesome experiences!

We then drove to Los Angeles. I did not like "the City of Angeles." Too crowded for me. From there we drove to Las Vegas, the city of lights and slot machines. I didn't enjoy Las Vegas as I thought it was too "plastic," like not real, and the sounds of the slot machines were annoying. Since that visit, I have gone back once and changed my opinion about it; it is still annoying but very nice to visit.

From Los Vegas we flew to the Grand Canyon in a very small plane. The view was breath-taking and once on the ground, the tranquility of the desert was overwhelming. Definitely a place to experience!

Every time we went on vacation, at least for the first two days, I felt still mentally connected to my office. However, thereafter I couldn't pronounce the name of my employer!

The best of all my trips happened when I retired in 2015. I rented a house in Positano-Italy. Together with my sons Eddie and his then wife Ashleigh, Eddy and his now wife Patty, plus Tommy Mendez my godson, and Valentina my niece flew there. We spent 10 days admiring the gorgeous view of the Amalfi Coast, on the southern coast of Italy. Positano with its winding roads, multiple stores and restaurants adorning the road, took us from the top of the mountain, where the house was located to a beautiful deep dark blue Mediterranean Sea.

Every day, we walked from the house, all the way to the beach. Of course, we stopped on our way down and up to enjoy an Italian gelato, the best in the world. We kept saying, "one *gelato* per day keeps the doctors away".

One day, we all decided to rent a boat, exclusively for ourselves. The captain took us to the Blue Grotto, a magnificent cave where the sun's light navigates its way to illuminate the bottom of the cave. This causes the color of the water to become sparkling light blue. Amazing site!

Each day we dinned in a different restaurant and enjoyed the Italian food at its best. This trip was a great opportunity to celebrate my retiring after 40 years in the Corporate world!

Learning First

My sisters and I went to the same school, "San Jose de Tarbes," except for Blanca who attended "Colegio La Consolación". Usually, in my country, we stay in the same school from pre-K to high school. The difference from the USA is that schools are not necessarily in the same neighborhood but across town away from each other. As we moved around Caracas, on some occasions, my school was 30 mins away from our home.

As our school was run by nuns, the religious values we acquired there complimented very well the ones we experienced at home. The invaluable bonds we developed with our classmates have remained intact.

I graduated from High School in July 1969. Just recently that class celebrated our 50th anniversary. Although I couldn't travel to Caracas, a group of my classmates who were able to leave the country flew to Miami, Florida and joined those of us who live here to celebrate the occasion. A nice lunch in downtown Miami was the center of our celebration. Two of my visiting classmates and I had not seen each other in fifty years. Yet, without losing a bit, our feelings picked up our friendship where we left it fifty years ago.

When I was in High School, my dream was to become an engineer. All the tests administered by the school and my meetings with the student's counsellor confirmed my academic aspiration. After attending a pre-admission program during the summer, I was admitted to the Universidad Católica Andres Bello in Caracas. At that time, some forty years ago, the University was about 25 minutes from my parents' house. Nowadays, with traffic, it could be around 90 minutes or more.

My sister Pachy and I shared a Volkswagen to go to college or some of my friends picked me up at home, if our schedules didn't match. On campus, I was very lucky because my high school friend Chicho Martorano and I were in the same program. We would spend the entire day together, escaping our friend Irene who was always in charge of keeping Chicho and I focused on following the study schedule.

One day, during a summer program, I was attending class and the guy seated next to me asked me if my name was Morella

Echenagucia. Before I answered, I looked at him and almost screamed "are you Luis Parilli?" He and I were best friends in kindergarten but hadn't seen each other in 13 years. It was a very sweet reunion. Many years after this encounter, we found out that his son and my son were best friends in primary school. Isn't that something?

Over 40 years ago, it was not common for women to study engineering. We were very few women during the first two semesters of college, maybe not more than twenty among 1000 plus students. The guys were wild and we were a bit overwhelmed by the attention we got. It was during our second semester when three girls decided to wear pants and not skirts. A big revolution at that time, and almost a sin to go to college wearing pants. Once the first group showed up in pants, everybody in the University followed, but not before the entire University criticized us for having the nerve to break up an unwritten rule. Nowadays, students attend class in "bermudas" and flip flops during summertime.

After the first full year, I decided to enroll in a summer program to stay ahead of Calculus courses. The program started in early August. During the first week of class, all of a sudden, I felt a very strong pain in my lower back. My friend Ernesto Galdo drove me home as I couldn't even drive. Long story short, a few days later I had surgery to remove a pilonidal cyst. Unfortunately, the university bursar office didn't reimburse me the tuition since the program had already started when I withdrew from it.

After two full semesters, I realized engineering was not for me. I was in a group study time at my friend Chicho's house when unexpectedly, I communicated to them that I was dropping out of the engineering program. They were in shock. Chicho and I always studied with Ernesto Galdo and Gustavo Penzo; the four of us were inseparable. I just couldn't handle it anymore. It was February 1971. They all tried to convince me to stay in the program. However, it was going to be too painful for me as I already was disenchanted with the subject matter and its requirements.

In retrospect, I think two aspects impacted my decision. One, and I think this was the most important, I found the subjects were too dry, far away from the human aspect. Secondly, because I never got a failing grade in high school and now at the university my grades were very poor even though I studied hard. The problem was how to explain it to my dad!

Even though my parents had limited schooling, they were very demanding when it came to education. My dad used to say: "education is the only thing you will inherit, take it, or leave it!" Both parents encouraged us to excel in what we did and to obtain a very good education. At the end of each school year, during the students' performance recognition event, my five older sisters with their medals of honor would be called to the stage to recognize the single family with the most medals of honor. The equivalent of a "B minus" was a royal sin at home! I was a regular sinner during my years in primary school but learned my lessons and repented during High School years.

My parents' biggest pride was when they were asked about their daughters. They enjoyed saying that Kico graduated Summa Cum Laude, Yolanda was an Economist, Lilian a lawyer, Pachy, and Morella "licenciadas" in Industrial Relations and Carolina a language therapist for children with disabilities. My parents really made a big effort to send all of us to college. We all attended college except for two of my sisters who married after High School: Blanca the oldest, and Mariela the third.

When I decided to quit engineering, I called my sister Kico first asking for her advice about how to tell dad. She advised me to see my dad with a plan about what to do next. "Don't just tell him you are dropping off but go to him with a plan", she said. I went to see him terrified by what his reaction was going to be. I felt I had failed him, and I didn't want to hurt him. The conversation was easier than I expected. He said he wanted me to be happy and enjoy what I was going to do as a professional. He reminded me that I dropped out of engineering but not college. Huff!

I decided to take English classes until the next college period. The problem was that I didn't know what to study next, but I promised him that I was going back to college. I was absolutely sure, but I was totally disoriented about what to study next. He accepted the plan and the pressure began!

I took two months of English, two hours three days a week, but unfortunately, the time to enroll in a new career came back too soon! I admit that the time with only a few hours a week at the English Lab was great, especially after the brutal time I spent every day studying engineering. Few days before the start of the semester, I had no clue what discipline to select. Again, my sister Kico suggested Human Resources. This happened to be her area of study, as well as my sister Pachy. So I did. No thinking process at all, just the fear of not having a clear inclination to a particular professional career and having my dad constantly on my back.

An area of study chosen out of desperation, considering my dad's demand, led to a career that fitted me like a glove. In retrospect, I think the study of human resource management (HR) was the beginning of my desire to serve others and be balanced in life. In the corporate environment, the HR job is supposed to be the bridge between the company and the employees. I developed a soft but firm personality. I placed myself in people's shoes and considered every person's situation before acting upon it. I really enjoyed every HR job I had during forty years of work. There were many cases when I had to firmly defend an employee and many others when I felt the company was right and I had to explain and convince employees about it. I practiced fairness, honesty, and determination.

My first job was with a local reinsurance company in Venezuela. I was only a few days out of college when I was offered the Human Resources Head position. The company was very small, only 200 employees but I was managing all aspects of its HR. My career was very unique because I started at the top of the chain of command within HR; however, I had no one to learn from, which was not good, but I survived. I recall calling my sisters, Kico and Pachy, many times asking for advice. They were very generous and helpful to me.

After three years with the company, I was going through the failure of my marriage. I was just 25 years old, and with a two-year-old son. At that time, the Venezuelan government was sponsoring scholarships to continue education in the USA, "Becas Mariscal de Ayacucho" was the name of the program. My friend from college, Marlene Hernandez, wanted to apply and asked me to go with her to the government agency to fill out the application. She insisted that I apply too, so I did with no expectations at all. A few weeks later, I was surprised when I got a call congratulating me on being admitted into the program. I was very happy but very scared at the same time.

After consulting with my parents, I decided to accept the scholarship and go to the USA. I tendered my resignation to my boss Eduardo Wallis, who was the President of the company. He didn't accept my resignation but instead, he gave me a leave of absence and a $200 monthly support. Over forty years ago, this amount was a lot. It was very generous of him and a big help for me, especially knowing that I would have a job coming back. I will always be grateful to him.

After my brother in law Orlando intervened, my then ex-husband gave his approval to allow me to take my son out of the country so I could complete a master's degree in Industrial Relations, with the caveat that his approval was only for one-year max. Having a master's degree in my resume had been a door opener from then on!

The program offered the opportunity to select the state and city in the USA. I selected Cleveland to improve my English skills before entering graduate school because I thought that city was going to be all Americans and no Latinos. I guess I was not original in choosing Cleveland as many other Venezuelans had thought about the same. My building was full of Venezuelans! I tried to be a bit distant from them to work on my English skills. I was cordial but not intimate with the Venezuelans in my building. I didn't want to be every moment surrounded by Spanish speaking people because I was very committed to learning English in just a few weeks.

Marcel and I arrived in Cleveland at the end of August 1979, after spending two weeks with my sister Blanca in Florida. I don't have words to describe how I felt to be with a two-and-a-half-year-old child in the remote and freezing weather of Cleveland. The weather was so miserable there that people stayed at home, the streets were deserted, and days and days were overcast or snowing. Over forty years have passed, and I have not found a reason to go back and visit this city. Sorry, Cleveland for the bad press!

I rented a one-bedroom apartment not far from the school. I bought a box spring and a mattress from a local store, a table with three chairs from the Salvation Army, and a few kitchen utensils from a convenience store.

I started looking for a daycare for Marcel but there were none available. I visited one that belonged to Case Western Reserve University, where I was enrolled to start English courses. Some of my new friends had discouraged me because they had not been able to have their children admitted. The admission officer told me they didn't have availability. I was under much pressure, so I started crying. She looked at me and gave me the admission right away. Tears sometimes help!

The first week I used public transportation, but the segregation between the people of color and whites was too much for me to bear; so was the people openly smoking pots on the bus. I was coming from Venezuela, where at that time marihuana was not common. Literally, I got off the bus, stopped at a car dealer, and bought a mustang for $6000, using credit for the first time in the USA. This was the price of a Ford Mustang over forty years ago! I wish I could have it back now. I bet it could fetch me a fortune!

Cleveland represented my first interaction with the concept of diversity. At that time, we had lots of schoolmates from Iran and the Middle East. One evening, one of the students from Saudi Arabia found my phone number and called to inform me that he was going back home in few days and "he had made the decision" to select me as his future wife so he wanted me to accompany him to Saudi Arabia to meet his family! I don't know how I managed to hold my surprise and laugh while explaining to him that in my culture we are not "picked" as a wife. Never mind the explanation of the concept of love and how the decision to get married is primarily made jointly by the couple. He was in shock that I turned down his offering as apparently, he came from a renowned and rich Saudi family and for some women back home it would have been an honor to be picked! Oh well, I guess you cannot win them all!

Eventually, after several minutes, we finished the conversation with my Saudi suitor. He never said hello to me again.

At the time I was studying English, I took the GMAT, GRE, and Toefl tests, and applied to universities in the New York City (NYC) area. I had already contacted my friend from college Adriana Mendoza and her husband

Cesar Miguel Rondon. The two had relocated from Venezuela to Manhattan, the heart of New York City. Adriana introduced to the one-year program offered by Pace University- Lubin School of Business. I had applied to Cornell University and they had sent me an acceptance letter for the next fall semester. Unfortunately, I couldn't wait that long because I only had one year to go back to Venezuela.

Test results were going to be ready in early January. I didn't have the admission yet, but I was sure it was going to come. Then I decided to move to NYC in December and wait for the results. This was the attitude of a real ignorant in the USA universities' admission process! What can I say?

At the end of my English language program, my parents traveled to Cleveland in early

December 1979 to help us move to NYC. The trip started at around 2 pm on Dec 13th in the middle of a huge snowstorm. I was driving with a small U-Haul trailer connected to my car. It was a royal nightmare. I never drove one before and especially in the middle of a snowstorm. To drive straight was not the problem but parking was a different story. It took us around ten hours to arrive in New York. We decided to rest a few miles from the city at a road hotel. We finally entered NYC in the morning hours.

We entered via the George Washington bridge. When I felt myself driving through Broadway with the trailer and trying to stop at the hotel, I almost freaked out!

I dropped off my parents and Marcel at the hotel and continued to my new friend Simone's apartment. There, I dropped off the contents of the trailer, basically suitcases, kitchen utensils, books, and few more items.

The problem at Simone's home was that the building was in the middle of a park. I couldn't park next to it but to carry everything all by myself to the building and then upstairs to her place. Later, I returned the trailer.

I decided to spend 1979 Christmas with my parents family in Caracas. I totally convinced myself that I was going to be admitted to the University upon my return to New York in January 1980. Positive attitude, a crazy risky girl, or a total ignorant? All of the above for sure!

After spending a nice Christmas Holiday with my family, I left Marcel with my parents and returned to NYC the day before the start of the semester class at Pace University, Lubin School of Business. At that time, I had already received the test results, however, I later found out that the university had not received the original test transcripts. The head of the international student's admission office told me that unfortunately, they didn't have the originals yet, so I couldn't start during the spring semester. If I couldn't be enrolled in the university at that time, the Venezuelan government would have withdrawn the scholarship. So, I had to fight for "my life" or be sent back to my country. I don't know what I said to the admission officer, but I convinced her to approve it and I started classes that same day, January 29th, 1980. Obviously, this event happened over forty years ago. Now the admission processes have changed. I cannot imagine a case like this in today's world.

My scholarship was $465 plus my dad's contribution of $250 and the $ 200 from my company made up my monthly budget of $915. The rent in Stuyvesant Town on first avenue and 20th street in Manhattan was $450 and Marcel's daycare was $160. The rest, $315, was for transportation, food, clothes, medicines, and entertainment. I never felt tight in funding. Marcel and I enjoyed all the free parks around NYC. Our mother-son relationship grew stronger and stronger. We only had each other, and we enjoyed our time together.

The car I had bought in Cleveland was not needed in NYC. Unfortunately, I had no choice but to sell it. The car had depreciated by some 40% from what I paid in Cleveland.

So, when I sold it, I accepted around 40% price reduction from the original price. It hurt a lot but parking garages in NYC were very expensive and street parking a royal nightmare, not to mention the vandalizing of cars.

We lived in the same neighborhood as my new friend Simone Yoshimoto. She had a long-term friendship with my family. Even though I just met her, Simone and I started a close relationship that has lasted ever since. Simone was and still is my friend, my sister, my proofreader for my Master program thesis, a great adviser, and a great human being. We always "fight" for non-sense matters such as who pays the bill when we go out as we both want to pay. While my rental was ready to be occupied, I stayed at her place for about two weeks.

Simone had a small Australian parrot bird called Jacko, that she had spent hours and hours training on how to talk and ask for a kiss. He was flying freely around the apartment, with no cage. I had always been afraid of flying creatures. One day, I was alone at her apartment studying for my next assignment, and Jacko flew over me to my shoulders. I was so scared and annoyed by the bird constantly asking, yes, for a kiss. I had no option but to lock him up inside the kitchen not knowing that few mins after my thoughtful decision, Simone was coming back home. Even today we both laughed about how serious she was when she found Jacko locked in the kitchen. "This is Jacko's home," she said! Oops!

A few days later I moved to the new apartment and right there my mom and

Marcel arrived. It was February 1980, one of the coolest months of the year and sure enough Marcel got very sick with a high fever. I missed two days of class. On the third day, my mom encouraged me to attend class, so I went. In the middle of the class, I was informed by a security guard that I had an urgent phone call. I left the class and took the call. It was from the hospital. The doctor was trying to explain to me that Marcel had a seizure and they needed my authorization to perform a spine test for meningitis. I closed my eyes, did a short prayer, and gave my authorization while I run to the hospital in midtown. It was the New York University Medical Center on first avenue and 31st St.

By the time I got there, the test has been performed and the results were negative. The high fever was the cause of the seizure.

Thank God it never happened again but as a prevention, he was medicated for the next few years, which made him a bit hyperactive. Oh boy!

My mom later told me that when Marcel started to convulse, she was praying when Simone, our Japanese/French/American friend knocked at the door and immediately went with them to the hospital. My mom did not speak a word of English and she wouldn't have known where to go and how to reach me at school; there were no cell phones at that time, but as always God was on our side.

After this event, I mentioned to my mom that maybe I had to go back to Venezuela given Marcel's recent medical condition. She didn't say anything but obviously, she referred our conversation to my dad. The following day he called me and gave me one of his most memorable lessons. He didn't make any reference to the comments I made to my mom. He only said: "when you left alone with Marcel to the USA, you broke my heart. The only thing that has kept me going is thinking about the day when you will come back with the diploma in your hands." That was enough for me!

In other words, don't let obstacles stop your goals in life, fight for it! It was the last time I thought about going back. Lessons learned, message received, and copied!

I enrolled Marcel in a local day-care very close to our place, but my classes started from 6 pm to 10 pm so I needed a babysitter for that period. One day, I saw a girl with several children entering the building and asked her if she would be interested to babysit Marcel. She was very happy to have a steady babysitter job. Her name was Susan, she was 16 years old. She used to pick up Marcel and take him to her parents' home two floors above our place. They loved and "adopted" Marcel and I was very happy to know that Marcel was secure at their place with adults. Susan took care of Marcel until we left NYC to return home. Her mom was a photographer and she took several pictures of Marcel that I have kept over the years.

I always have had the feeling that God has a special blessing for me. Throughout my life, he has always shown me His presence. He has constantly guided me through every challenge I have encountered in my life. It is like I am in free-falling when He comes to my rescue. Never abandoned me, permanently on my side. What am I without Him?

During the time in New York, I had the blessing of having my friend Adriana and her then-husband Cesar Miguel as my family. Adriana and I were in the same master's program at the same university. We became very close friends and as a matter of fact, the three of us became Marcel's parents. Many times, Cesar took Marcel to movies or parks to allow Adriana and me to spend time studying. Many times, the three of us attended parents' meetings. Many times, Adriana took control of the situation and negotiated with Marcel to open his mouth to eat because we were late to go to class. This was hilarious! At that time Marcel only ate oatmeal, french fries, "arepa" with butter, and blended vegetable soup. However, in many instances, he refused to open his mouth and Adriana started her daily speech to convince him to eat.

As soon as I completed my Master's degree program and before I returned to Venezuela I married Odoardo Carta, my second husband. We had been dating for two years. We were married at the town hall in NYC. My mom, Adriana, and Cesar attended. My dad and my oldest sister Blanca and her husband Raul came to New York for the wedding. Unfortunately, due to scheduling complication they left before the wedding.

Getting a civil wedding in NYC was so different than in Venezuela. We bought in advance the marriage license for $5 and went for a required medical examination. After that and without any appointment we showed up at the Town Hall with our marriage license. Once in line, the judge called for the next couple. We entered his office. He recited some phrases that we hardly heard and with a *sotto-voce* said: "you may kiss the bride, NEXT!" That was it. We were officially married. The next couple entered his office!

After the honeymoon, I went back to the reinsurance company for two additional years. A new President from Germany had replaced Eduardo Wallis. It was hard to work with him. His management skills and practices and mine were poorly aligned. I resigned and accepted a job at Citibank.

At Citibank my career took off on a different path. I traded in being head of a mouse for being in-charge of the tail of a lion!

From the bottom up

My job for the most part, was always international. I travelled to major cities in Latin America, Europe and some countries in South Asia such as Singapore, Malaysia and also to Australia.

Some people thought my job was very glamorous because it was international. In reality, I enjoyed traveling to other locations because of the variety of cultures and issues. A particular topic would have had different answers based on the culture of the country. I enjoyed international travelling, but, really? Glamorous? After 9/11, traveling became a major headache. The world was never the same and such was the glamorous aspect of traveling! TSA became a royal pain and the rest is history!

As far as I remember, from all the multiple trips I took during my professional life, it was only in Mexico City, Singapore and Australia that I added one day to my business schedule to tour around.

I went to Mexico to conduct a training program to Citibank employees. I arrived a day before the start of the program. I took a tour to the Pyramids of the Sun and the Moon located in Teotihuacan, the famous Zona Rosa, The Zocalo and the Palacio de Bellas Artes, where I saw the Folkloric Mexican Ballet, all in one day! During the week I was there, one evening I had the opportunity to visit the famous Plaza Garibaldi, where countless groups of "Mariachis" tried to catch the attention of tourists for a good tip. Beautiful plaza but very scary because every group of Mariachis did everything possible to get closer to tourists before others.

It was during this first trip to Mexico when I found out that some Spanish words had very different meanings depending on cultures. Unfortunately, it was too late when in my opening statement the eyes of the locals were in shock after I said what I said. As I realized what had happened, I decided to present a "disclaimer" saying "sorry guys, we share the same language, but some words have different meanings". We all laughed. Phew!

In Singapore, I travelled with a friend who worked in our London office. After such a long trip we did not want to miss the opportunity to visit some landmarks around the city. Although exhausted, we decided to take a shower before venturing out. We took a tour around the city and had so much fun. The Garden by the Bay, the Helix bridge, Clarke Quay, Chinatown and so much more were astonishing! The following day, we attended the global meeting even though our eyes were closing for the next day or two.

In Sydney, I also was with a coworker and again we decided to take a tour, even though we couldn't differentiate day from night after 22 hours flight. It was a beautiful city specially the famous Opera House, the Sydney Harbour Bridge, the Royal Botanic Garden and the Darling Harbour. Locals were very friendly with a very different English accent.

Interesting to mention Tokyo-Japan. One of the days at the office, there was a gathering with all employees in a beautiful

Japanese garden. People at the office prepared a typical Kimono dress for my coworker and for me. It also included the socks and the wooden shoes that looked like flip-flops. They had to dress us because the Kimono had many pieces. It takes experience in how to put it together. We couldn't be happier to mingle with the employees sharing parts of their culture. It was a great experience.

In Tokyo I did not add any extra day but the day we were returning to the US, very early in the morning, I received a call from my son Eduardo, who was in NYC. He asked me what I have seen so far. I said we didn't have time to tour the city. He said "mom, you can't come back if you don't visit the Shibuya crossing, the wildest crossing in the world. When I said I didn't have the time and that in few hours I had a working lunch and right after I was going to the airport, he almost fainted! "Mom, you cannot leave Tokyo if you don't go there". Well, I had no option but to move the lunch up one hour and asked the driver to take me there before dropping me off at the airport. It was worth it. Japanese are very gentle in their demeanors; the crossing is very civilized and wild at the same time. I don't know how many people were crossing in different directions and nobody hit anybody. How they do it? It is a Japanese mystery!

I visited Brazil many times, both Sao Paulo and Rio de Janeiro. In Rio, I never went up to the see the famous Christ the Redeemer. In retrospect, it was a shame, I missed many opportunities to tour the cities I visited for business, but in reality, after working the entire week with meetings and diners, etc. I just wanted to get on the plane and comeback home.

I learned to travel light with a carry on, good for an entire week. I used to travel with matching shoes and handbags. However, experience taught me that I only needed one pair of working shoes and had all outfits combined with that color. Usually, two pants or skirts and 5 matching tops for a working week were enough.

I only recall one or two challenging incidents during heavy time of traveling. Trips to Latin America usually included visits to several countries in one packed week. The first country to visit in one of my Latin American trips was Brazil. I arrived at the hotel in Sao Paulo at around 11 am, after a 10-hour flight from NYC and the usual traffic jam from the airport to the city. I took a shower and was getting ready to go to the office when I realized I had packed outfit tops but had left at home skirts or pants to go with them! I got in panic because I only had three hours before my first meeting. I called a friend from the office and she directed me to a nearby mall. I had to run out quickly and shop before a meeting that was scheduled for 2pm! I only bought a black skirt, twice the price I would have paid in NYC, but I had no option. I wore the same skirt for the next five days!

During the same trip, after two days I continued to Argentina. The day I was leaving from Argentina to Chile, I checked out from the hotel to go to the local office first before going to the airport. Taxis in Buenos Aires are black with yellow strips, same colors but slightly different from those of the hotel which are yellow with black strips. I hailed a taxi thinking that taxi was from the hotel, big mistake! I placed my carry on in the front seat. The driver started a conversation about how one of his sons was dying while his wife was battering breast cancer. Not to mention that the night before after a full working day, he was robbed and now he had no money at all. His story was very emotional to the point I found myself crying with him, literally!

As soon as we arrived at the office, I paid him substantially more to support him but as soon as I closed the rear door, he drove off with my carry on. In my mind, I thought "he is going to come back because he is a good man and he just didn't realize my carry on was next to him". I waited several minutes but he never came back. Well, I later found out, this was their MO to rob women under emotional distress. I couldn't believe I had been part of a hoax because I always thought I was very sharp and aware of risky situations. My co-workers in Argentina used to tease me saying that a driver had stopped in the office looking for a Venezuelan woman under emotional stress. Not funny!

Being three more days away from going back home, I had no choice but to run to the famous "Calle Florida" in Buenos Aires and shop from a toothbrush to a carry-on bag. Over fifteen years have passed and I still have the same bag, made of Argentinian leather, the best! Shopping follows me, more than I follow it, yeah right! Calle Florida is a very beautiful place, full of shops and restaurants.

Traveling for business alone, had many benefits, especially if no business dinners were "on the menu". My dream had always been to get to the hotel, showering and ordering room service while watching a movie or the news; totally disconnecting from the business! I missed my family but time all by myself was always priceless. In addition, one of the attractions of traveling alone, was the time I spent meditating. The day-to-day activities plus the family and the normal chores at home, usually took time away from me.

One night, many trips after the famous trip I mentioned earlier, I was in Buenos Aires at the very nice Hyatt Hotel, near Patio Bullrich mall. I had spent the entire day in meetings from morning to late afternoon. As soon as I arrived at the hotel, I ordered my favorite room service, which was onion soup, apple pie and a glass of Argentinian white wine. After watching the news, I decided to go to bed. Few minutes after, I was doing my nightly devotions and became very absorbed in my prayers. The level of concentration I had that night had never happened to me before. I realized I was very emotional as I was asking the Lord that I wanted to see His eyes, His face, for only a second. For the first time in my life, I heard Him saying to me "if you want to see my eyes, look around to the people in need". I remembered the famous painting of the face of Jesus that at a closer look, it was composed by numerous faces of people. His face He said, was the face of all those people in my life, known and unknown. The everyday brother or sister I could see everywhere. This was quite an experience! I got goose bumps with my emotions to the roof!

It was difficult to fall sleep. My mind was reviewing family, friends, co-workers and people in general, the ones I liked and those I didn't like. Have I seen them as if they were Jesus? I didn't think so. There were people I liked and people I disliked or tried to avoid. People who had loved me and people who had hurt me in one way or the other. I was very intolerant to people who were rude or lazy or people just different than me in thoughts or attitude. I used to judge people even before I gave them a chance. Many times, I saw people in the office or in social events that I had never shared a hello with and yet, I did not like them. Maybe they were too loud or dressed different or what have you. Maybe I thought that if they were different than me, they were wrong. I was full of pride.

I think that what I experienced in Buenos Aires was very powerful; however, I went on with my life and even though I always remembered this occasion with emotions I only made few adjustments to my interaction with others. I mean, I was always nice to people and if someone needed me, I was there to help out but that was it. I did not reach out to people in need, people came to me for help and I helped, but I never went the extra-mile.

To explain my international career, I have to go back to my time at Citi-Venezuela from 1983 to 1999.

My career at Citi-Venezuela grew very fast. I started as the head of Training and Development and in less than a year, my job was expanded to include Recruitment and Selection, and a year later I also headed Compensation and Benefits.

I made good friends in Human Resources Management (HR) and across the company. Specially in HR I made great friends like Aintzane de Brabo with her strong Spanish "z" accent and funny stories, Elenita Monasterios with whom I shared the same birthday and Marianela Ruiz, whose laugh and great personality were a magnet to the entire bank. These are friendships for life. Marianela and I became very close and our laughers were contagious. We travelled together within the country and Europe. Unfortunately, Marianela left us too early but she is in my heart where she continues to accompany me.

There were many more friends across other areas of the bank. Gisela Sucre, who lived in the same neighborhood where I lived, far from the bank. We used to ride together once or twice a week. Our friendship has continued in the US and my children have always seen her as part of the family.

Even though I was almost managing the entire HR function, at one point my boss in HR was removed and the job was not offered to me. Someone from the business, who had highly criticized the role of HR got the job. I was extremely disappointed and ready to resign. After several calls from the Head of HR from NYC, the Citibank Consumer Bank head offered me the Branch Manager role of the largest Citi branch in Caracas. I decided to accept it and moved on with a twist in my career; from HR to the front line.

I had no previous experience selling the most expensive bank products to very demanding clients. I studied every product in detail and had the benefit of leading a great group of individuals willing to support my learning curve. In return, I offered my organization and strategic approach. In a year time, we went from being a group to becoming a strong and cohesive team. I really enjoyed the experience; actually, I firmly believe every HR person should have the experience of working in a frontline job to learn about the business and understand its challenges. I was devastated when I did not get the HR head job, but God had a better plan for me as this opportunity to work on the business side elevated my career at a more strategic level and made me more "marketable" for future jobs.

A year later, the new head of HR decided to quit HR; it was easier to challenge HR from the outside than when leading HR. I found out the President was interviewing outside candidates. I think he sent me the head of the Investment Bank to inform me about his intentions so as to test my desire to go back to HR. In any case, I was not going to miss the opportunity to fight for what I considered to be mine. After all, HR was my passion. I went and met the President of Citi-Venezuela. I told him: "..there are other qualified professionals in the market but none of them has the knowledge of the bank that I have. I don't need to be trained. I can produce now". The rest is history, I got the job!

Tom Charters was the President and up to this day we have continued our friendship. Thereafter, he has been my mentor throughout my professional career.

The people we hired at that time had just come back after finishing their MBA in USA. Others were already professional employees in the market but all of them had the distinctive Citi profile: creative, driven, committed and fun to work with. Those years are gone because the employee-company relationships have been re-defined to a more distant and transactional one.

This time as the head of HR for the country was very attractive and challenging at the same time. The inflation rate in Venezuela was between 50 to 60%, with an exceptional peak of 100% in 1996. The percentage of people living in poverty rose to 66% in 1995.

We had to be creative to increase employees' income without a high impact on the bank's liabilities. A bonus was added to their salaries with no impact on employees' taxes. We created a win-win for all. We also negotiated with the bank to pay the year-end bonus in US dollars rather than in Venezuelan Bolivares. This was a big hit for the employees.

At year end when the "utilidades" or special Christmas bonus were paid, all employees came to the HR department where we had music, hot chocolate and the delicious Pan de Jamon, typical in Venezuela during Christmas time. The comradery, support and commitment found at all levels were impactful and I had not seen it in other companies I worked after Citi-Venezuela

After few years in this role, Tom Charters retired and Mike Contreras became the Regional Head of Citi, based in Caracas. Mike was from Puerto Rico and he and his family had been in Venezuela before. I was very happy as we were already good friends. Mike named me the head of HR for the Andean Region. After few years Mike and his family were transferred to Asia and my intentions to continue my career elsewhere increased. Finally, by the end of 1996, I was offered a role in NYC, as the Global Head of HR for Derivatives, Sales and Trading.

In total, I worked at Citi-Venezuela for over twelve years until the day of my transfer to NYC. During my farewell party, I received many demonstrations of love and good wishes. The biggest surprise came from the wife of the head of the Union, who made me a bag for my trip. Coming from the Union its value was exponential. Over the years I developed with the Union a very respectful and thrustful relationship. The Citi sport club that I encouraged and supported during my tenure, also gave me a recognition plaque. It was hard to leave even though I was excited about the new life for my family and the career opportunities presented to me.

The professional family life at Citi-Venezuela was very strong and up to this day the relationships have continued across country boundaries.

My international career was boosted from the moment I was transferred by Citibank from Venezuela to NYC. At that time my career aspiration was to spend 2-3 years in NYC and then Asia! Funny to remember that the day after my family and I arrived at NYC, we went to Chinatown. That day coincided with the Chinese market on the streets. Streets were packed, the traffic was horrible, vendors everywhere, pedestrian sorting out the cars in a bumper-to-bumper nightmare. After dealing with this headache, my son Eddie said to me "Mom, are you sure you want to go to Asia after NYC". We all laughed out loud as maybe for them it was not a good idea!

My legal status in the USA was tied up to the bank; I had an L-1 visa and my husband wasn't authorized to work in the US. Nevertheless, we agreed that to give our children a better future the journey to the US was the best choice for the family.

We settled in Darien, CT. a very small town 55 minutes by Metro North train from NYC. Schools were great and the town was very supportive of children in sports and my two boys were very much into sports. It was my husband though, who attended parents' meetings at school or my children's sports activities as I was working in NYC all day long.

Citi assigned a third-party company to help us with the day-to-day basics and extremely necessary tasks such as getting a driver's license or enrolling our children to schools, etc. That person was who later turned out to be my dearest friend Diane Roth. She and her husband Alfredo became instantly part of our family. Many times in the years to come, we travelled together and shared many moments that will always stay in our hearts. Alfredo is swiss with a Spaniard mom, Diane is American, and both spoke many languages including Spanish.

It was not all roses; even though I continued to work for the same company in a different country, the working environment, cultural differences, and everything in between were very challenging. Working at Citi Venezuela or working at Citi NYC was a totally different story. The first cultural difference was at the elevators. No eye contact, no hello at all. On the train, same train every day, same car, same people and not even eye contact. At the office, very formal and cautious with what you say and to whom you say it. The business in general was very competitive, less friendly and more focused on individual's own achievements. It was not an environment conducive to trust or support on each other. Even though I was very enthusiastic about working in NYC, deep in my heart I missed the collaboration and friendly environment of Citi-Venezuela.

As soon as I arrived at the office, I found out that my boss was leaving. The business was new to me, which did not bother me at all but the knowledge of the internal politics was kind of a nightmare. I replaced her for few weeks until the new head arrived. She was a Canadian woman, very smart but very insecure. At a personal level she was great but as a boss she was a royal headache. She was later transferred back to Canada and I assumed her role.

Every evening I walked from Park Avenue and 51th St. to Grand Central Station on 42nd St. Just having the former Pan-Am building now the Met-Life building in front of me and seeing all those tall buildings along the avenue, made me feel so lucky. I was working in what was considered the center of the world and there I was with a luggage full of goals and wishes for a better future for my family and me. How many people in my country would have liked to be where I was? The opportunities I had had in my life had been unique; only because the Lord has guided me since I was born.

At the same time I was adjusting to the new working environment, my family was adjusting to live in Darien. The children loved their schools and after few days their English was definitely improving. Basically, I was working extensive hours while my husband and Leo, the nanny we brought from Venezuela, were taking care of the house and the children.

Sometimes I felt like a visitor at home. I was taking Metro North railroad at 6am and coming back at around 7-8 pm, every day. I missed many baseball games and parents' meetings during my professional life. Unfortunately, I was the bread winner, fortunately I had good jobs.

Few weeks after our arrival to USA, my dad had an emergency heart surgery. I urged to Caracas and was with him for one full week. I couldn't believe that something bad was going to happen to my dad and I was going to be far away. After a month of recovery, he couldn't wait to come and visit us at Rabbit Lane, our first house. It was a great opportunity for the children to be with their grandparents and particularly for me the opportunity to pamper them as much as I could. It was springtime. The house was surrounding by a beautiful garden with wildflowers and my favorite hydrangeas both blue and pink. Houses were very much separated from each other in distance with no fences in between. The first thing my dad did with the children was to ride a bike around the street. It was a cul-de sac so he enjoyed not having cars around; he was 83 years old at that time. Since that first year and for the next 15, my parents came to visit us every summer for a full month.

A year and a half after my transfer, Citibank was bought by Travelers; even though our CEO said it was a merge, there was not such a thing as a merge but a buy-out. With a duplication of jobs in certain areas, Travelers' HR took control and my job was going to be eliminated in a 6 month- period. I don't know how many resumes and interviews I had. I was in a difficult situation because I was not a resident yet but a visa holder tied to Citibank. The funny story was that one day I was walking on Park Avenue when I met Ricardo Ortega, a Citi-friend from Venezuela. He was working at UBS but he was looking for a job to go back to Venezuela. I gave him my resume and he gave me his. I gave his resume to TASA Consulting firm, who previously had called me for advice on candidates for a financial position job in Caracas. Ricardo introduced my resume to the UBS HR department. He got the Financial position job and I got the one at UBS. We used to laugh saying we helped each other out within the same resume exchange transaction!

In challenging moments, it is very difficult to keep our faith in God. On my shoulders I had my immediate family and the support I gave to my parents; I was really in dismay. It is good to remember that God never leaves us when we need him the most. His help did not come as I had wished, that a new job within the company be offered to me. Instead, He encouraged me to place my resume out there, to contact people I knew, etc. and wait for the best option yet. His plans are better than ours, always; However, God puts almost everything, and we put almost nothing, but God does not put his almost everything if we do not put our almost nothing.

One month before my termination day, UBS Bank, extended me an offer with their commitment to work on my US residence status. I went from desperation to heaven. It meant freedom to work for whoever I wanted, whenever I wanted. The new job was largely visible within the company and with extended geographic responsibilities throughout Latin America and NYC. Once again, I felt I was in freefalling when the Lord came to my rescue, never abandoned me, always on my side! I heard someone saying the following phrase that I really like and agree:

"Act as if everything depended on you but in desolation, trust as if everything were in God's hands"

I had been working for Citibank as an international staff and now I was hired by UBS as a local staff. It meant we needed to buy or rent a home as I no longer had rental house allowance paid by the company. At that time in Darien, the market was very "hot" and the inventory of houses available was very limited. We thought we had to move the children to new schools, which would have been a disaster for my children. Finally, we found a house across from Royle School at 23 Royle Road where Eddy was studying elementary school. The family sanity was kept intact! We lived there for a total of 12 years when we sold the house and moved to NYC.

Working for UBS proved to be interesting and challenging at the same time. While I was in the US or Latin America, my experience and enjoyment grew exponential, but when I had meetings in Switzerland it was a different story. I was the only woman reporting to the Global head of HR based in Switzerland, in addition of being a non-swiss and not a Swiss-German speaking. What a pain it was to be in a small room with all participants smoking and switching from English to Swiss-German every other minute! After few years, other women joined the team, but the smoking continued!

After working several years for UBS, I changed one more job to work at The Hartford in Hartford CT, before retiring from Experian Information Technology. The job at The Hartford was interesting but I had to drive one hundred miles each way. After three years, I couldn't do it anymore so I accepted the role offered by Experian, based in NYC. At that time my late husband's health was in accelerated decline. I decided to sell the house in Connecticut and move to an apartment in the upper west side in Manhattan in case of any emergency.

My last job at Experian was as the Senior VP Global Head of HR for Marketing Services Division. This job expanded my experience in every aspect and my geographic responsibilities including south Asia. In addition, my boss Mike DeVico, was very flexible and allowed me to work from home in Florida, when few years later my husband needed a warmer place to live and we bought a condo in Aventura-FL. Mike also travelled a lot and even though our common office was in NYC, he lived in Utah with his wife and commuted to NYC.

Every job I had while based in NYC, was better than the one before and they all came at the right time. It was like if every job I had was precisely selected by Him to provide me with the eventual freedom to retire and do His Will, as I did in 2015.

Even though through my career I was earning well, I have no idea how I managed to pay for a mortgage, my three sons' education, vacations, etc. with only one salary coming home. My family including my ailing husband, had no knowledge of the multiple actions I took to do all these. I realized that only with His blessings I was able to multiply my compensation and still able to save some. There were times when I thought the water was coming up to my neck, however, one way or the other eventually the water resided, and I was breathing again!

I never shared my anxiety with my husband, my children or anybody else. I kept every angst with myself, feeling it was my responsibility as "the family problem solver". I refinanced many times trying to keep cashflow at the level needed. I don't think my children realized the size of my responsibilities. I pretended everything was ok not to worry them. My husband never asked me for anything or worry about how or where the funds were coming from. I took control of the house and of the family. Many times I have regretted my attitude. Maybe, trying to avoid concerns on their side I kept them away from reality. I felt empty as many times I saw myself as a checkbook. It was not their fault I guess because it was my sole decision to keep problems away from them.

Just Recently, my youngest son Eduardo, sent me a Mother's Day gift with a card that read:

"Mom, when you thought I was not looking, I was. Thank you for the million ways you supported, encouraged, helped and loved me".

Even though I wasn't looking for recognition, it was very sweet to receive a note like this one that made me disregard the challenges I faced in the past. This note from him, made my all days to come.

Following my destiny

As my retirement days rolled alone, Uganda preoccupied my life...

After Malawi, the trip to Uganda was going to be about six months away, at the end of 2016.

Before my first trip to Uganda, I met an extraordinary woman, Elena Plaza. She asked me what I was going to do in Uganda. When I said I was going to work with women and children, she offered to train me in some sewing techniques. That way I could teach the women and help them establish some businesses. I thought it was a great idea, but I warned her that God gave me many talents but sewing was not one of them. She was very patient and generous with her time. She dedicated two full days training me. It wasn't an easy task as sewing doesn't come naturally to me. She persisted and, in the end, I enjoyed it. I became well versed in quilting, or so I boasted! Elena also bought everything I needed in Uganda for the training. I remember she inquired what was my budget. My answer was, "whatever you can fit in two suitcases". I was not allowed to take a third one unless I paid for it.

I had so many things to carry with me. I took clothes, toys, medicines, material for the sewing classes, my clothes, food, and more. I was a bit overwhelmed to start packing but my friends Blanca Salas, Adriana Mendoza, and Monica Villate came to my house and helped me pack everything. In the end, we realized I needed to add a third and a fourth suitcase. My friend Joan McCauley came to my rescue and paid for it. My belongings were in the carry-on, saving the suitcases for donations. I always travel with my "protein in a bottle," meaning peanut butter and small oatmeal packages. I never leave home without them! I am very particular when it comes to eating strange food; so, I ensure my protein intake won't suffer.

The trip to Uganda is a very long one. Door to door it is a 36-hour trip. Usually, it goes Florida—NYC—Brussels (or Amsterdam)—Kigali-Entebbe, Uganda. Entebbe airport is on the banks of Lake Victoria.

From Entebbe, there is a three to four-hour drive by car to Jinja. This depends on the notorious bumper-to-bumper traffic around Kampala, the capital.

On this trip I reunited in Brussels with my friend Jennifer Bernston, a nurse who I had met earlier in Malawi. At Entebbe, we met Bruce and his wife Pam McCormick. They were co-founders of Help International Primary School in Masese, Jinja.

Before heading to Jinja, we made a two-day detour to Buloba, southwest of Kampala. Here, we met Samson, a pastor, and friend of the couple. Samson was building a church in Buloba. It included a pre-K school they call Nazareth level.

After a bumpy ride to Buloba, we arrived at a hotel. It was situated close to Samson's project. Jenn and I shared a room at this hotel. It was clean and offered basic accommodation in an otherwise nice surrounding area.

The following day we went to visit the village where Samson and his family live. The church they were building was at that time a half-way-built shack.

It involved rudimentary construction. Builders used reeds and mud to construct walls. The entire structure was made up of just a roof and two mud walls plus additional sticks to help hold up the roof. The area was strikingly poor and relatively far from major towns. I was impressed to see Samson, his wife and two other pastors doing all they could to evangelize and baptize new Christians. There were no roads other than dirt and muddy paths. We walked with Samson to a well they have built for the neighbors to fill their containers with clean water. They had to carry the water over their heads back to the homes. Actually, the well was already there. What they did was build a protection wall around it to keep the water clean. The wall prevented animals from leaving their droppings in near the well.

There are many pastors in the area. Each one tries to do the best to spread the word of God. The area is also flooded with witchcraft practice. Therefore, the work of the pastors to evangelize the population was not an easy task. On the second day we went to a pool in the neighborhood. There, we found several people getting baptized as "Born again Christian". It was an amazing and different experience seeing the excitement of those being baptized inside the pool. We were deeply emotionally touched. My eyes were widely opened as I realized that Catholicism was not the only way to save and love people. The work these pastors were accomplishing in that part of the world was as loved by God as the one performed by Catholic priests elsewhere.

We also visited some humble shacks where people live. The roads were all muddy because of the rain. Their houses were very dark and hot. They comprised of one room where a family sits, eats, and sleeps. Children and parents, all in the same space. They cook outside of the house using charcoal. Latrines were outside the house. Their tiny and flimsy structures comprised of sticks covered with old rags to provide privacy, and often licking corrugated iron sheets for the roof. Flies were everywhere, even in people's faces. People didn't take any action to move or keep the flies away from their bodies. These people appeared powerless about their seemingly absurd poverty. Their children suffer from malnutrition, resulting in having big stomachs; many have malaria. They have no shoes, and their clothes were just rags. It was difficult to verbally connect with them, but their eyes reflected the plea for help that truly touched our hearts. We distributed some donations, medicines, and toys to the children.

Bruce and Pam have a long relationship with Samson. They sponsored him when he was a teenager. Samson had traveled to the USA, stayed at their home, and visited potential donors to support his ministry and eventually the construction of the school and church. As a matter of fact, several months after our visit, he got a substantial donation from the USA. This donation enabled him to build a solid structure for the church and the school.

The following day, we spent time with the children at the Nazareth school. This is the equivalent of a USA pre-K level. We sang songs and played with the children. Jenn ran a special workshop for women. She taught them the functioning of the human body and family planning options.

Later, we learned from Samson about a children sponsorship program he was using. It involved payment of school fees and some children essentials. I found this to be an effective way to raise funds to support needy children. One of the needy children Samson shared with us was Comfort. Carol was a single mom, at school studying to become a pastor, with a 6 years old daughter. The girl was living with Carol's mom and was lacking everything including a plain mattress. Getting a sponsor for Comfort would enable

Carol to focus on her education and eventually support her daughter. I was touched by the story of Carol and her daughter Comfort and decided to sponsor the child.

After two days in Buloba, we started our trip to Jinja about three hours away. The traffic was a nightmare. We became part of long lines of trucks and cars, people walking in the middle of the streets, moto-taxis or "boda-boda" as they are locally called, open-air street shops, animals, and every living creature. All appeared to share one rule: no one respected traffic rules. The perfect storm!

We arrived late in Jinja at the Nile hotel. Accommodations were modest but acceptable. We only wanted to rest and forget about everything else. I shared my room with Jen. The following day Jean Kaye arrived from Colorado.

HELP International Organization is based in Colorado. Jean Kaye and her husband are the CEO and CFO respectively of this global organization. The two plus Pam McCormick and her husband Bruce, and the couple of Delia, and Peter Garrity were the founders of HELP International Primary School in Masese, Jinja. I used the school as my center of operations in many of the subsequent trips to Uganda. It has an enrollment of around 600 children. Recently, they inaugurated a new two-story modern building.

After a nice rest, we were ready to hit the road! Breakfast was included. I learned to travel with my "protein in a bottle," peanut butter! So, I had a piece of bread with peanut butter, fruits, and water. The fruits in Uganda are very good, especially mangoes, papaya, pineapple, and sweet bananas. Even though I am not a fan of bananas, I became addicted to the sweet bananas. They are small but very sweet. There are many women on the streets of Jinja with their sweet banana baskets on their heads.

The Nile hotel is on the other side of the Nile river and the traffic to cross the bridge to Masese was always a headache. Jean and Jenifer were always obsessed with coffee, so we stopped at the Java café for them to recharge their daily batteries. I don't like coffee and have never drunk it. So, I had a great freshly squeeze orange juice.

The city of Jinja was built on the banks of the River Nile. It is here that the mighty river starts its long journey across many countries to its destination in the Mediterranean Sea. It was a delightful feeling to stand at source of this giant river. The view is breathtaking however the infrastructure is missing.

The Nile is the longest river in Africa. According to the Wikipedia, it is about 6,650 Km long and its drainage basin covers eleven countries: Tanzania, Uganda, Rwanda, Burundi, Congo, Kenya, Ethiopia, Eritrea, South Sudan, and Egypt. Its source comes from Lake Victoria (Blue Nile) and the primary stream of the Nile itself (White Nile). I have visited the source of the Nile many times, and the feeling of being on this famous river is amazing!

At daylight, I was surprised by the greenery of the place, the natural wonders are magic. Actually, Uganda is also known as the Pearl of Africa. I believe it was Winston Churchill who gave it that description. Uganda is a tropical country in east Africa.

In 1830, the British arrived looking for the source of the Nile and in 1894, Uganda became a British Protectorate. In 1870 Protestants and Catholics missionaries entered the country. In 1962 Uganda gained independence and became a member of the British Commonwealth. The current government has been in power for about 37 years and counting.

There are about 2.5 million children who had lost one or both parents, 1.5 million people infected with the HIV/Aids virus, and alcoholism is at 9%. Uganda is the African country with the most NGOs in the site. Corruption is rampant in much of the country.

When we arrived at the HELP International School in Masese we were in shock. Masese is a very impoverished area part of the District of Jinja. It used to be a place largely for immigrants from South Sudan and other neighboring countries. The population is about 14 thousand people, not confirmed. Some years ago, the Danish government invested in the area to support families to build their own houses. However, after frustration with the people, the Danish abandoned the project.

I was alarmed by my first sight of Masese. I saw naked children who seemed to be everywhere I looked; I saw lots of skinny goats, and some chickens desperately searching for what to eat, dirty uneven roads, cows in the middle of the road, trash everywhere, children scavenging for food, and air full of mosquitoes, transmitters of Malaria. Indeed, Masese was a heartbreaking place.

I have seen poverty in many Latin American countries, but this one was different. Power was limited to the very few who can afford it, water was carried on top of women's heads, from the well to their homes. I saw children who had not seen a good bath in months, many of them without shoes and many more without clothes. Their little faces were dirty but there was something in their eyes that was captivating. Those eyes talked about innocence and humility, all of them yarning for help but with a big smile on their faces.

After several trips to Masese I soon learned that when children see a white person, they immediately come right at us. I usually travel with candies in my backpack. Before I give away one, I must be sure I have plenty left because the entire village would soon follow. They like to touch our skin. I guess they think our skin color is fading. They also touch my elbow and play with my wrinkles. Sometimes I have five to eight children on each hand and a few more around my waist or legs. They are genuine, they are children with no filter!

As soon as we arrived at the school, we were introduced to the staff. Ronny Sitanga is the senior HELP International officer in Uganda. Richard Mugeni is the project manager; Ritah and Ben, are social workers; Robert is the purchasing officer; Arthur, IT director; Louis, team secretary, and Bonny Mukunja who does everything in between. Also, we met all the teachers.

Children were very happy to meet us and greeted us with their learned and practiced speech. They all recited it at the same time. When visitors entered their classes and said good morning children, how are you? They all responded, "we are humble and obedient." Even though they sound "cute" I didn't like it. The first time I heard them responding like that, I felt pain in my stomach. Students learned this greeting from the time Uganda was a British Colony. I felt this was a way to keep Ugandan children controlled and limited under the British regulations, hence limiting their creativity.

Many trips later, Jean invited Larry McEvoy, MD. He was an ER doctor but now his focus is to work on improving the analytical thinking of his fellow colleagues. He developed a methodology to analyze the same issue from different perspectives to obtain different results. Otherwise, if the same methodology is followed, every time the conclusion would be the same.

He applied his methodology to the teachers and administrative staff at the school's meetings and identified from the discussion other actions to implement. Subsequently, it was suggested to change the children's answers from "we are humble and obedient" to "we are humble, obedient and creative". Even though it was adding just one word, this meant a lot for the children's development. The teachers committed to giving children approval and encouragement to be curious and let their imagination do the rest. The school wanted to develop future talents and leaders and for this, changes needed to be introduced. Many other changes were introduced.

During my first trip, I divided my time between helping at school reading to the children, working with teachers, and selecting and training women using my newly acquired sewing techniques. I felt great having my own project with the women. Twenty of them received the training for two weeks. I promised to return in a few months and select the best to start off their new businesses. In the meantime, they were supposed to practice under the supervision of Ritah. She was responsible for taking care of the training material I had brought from America. I was thrilled, given my high expectations, thinking that these women were going to be able to financially sustain their families and have a way out of poverty.

This trip made a big impact on me. I was so moved and determined to support those women. I seriously considered postponing my already paid trip to Jerusalem and Petra with my sister Lilian. Jean convinced me to go ahead with my trip. She told me that we also needed to take care of ourselves.

Six months after my first visit, I decided to go back to Uganda and stay two months all by myself at a hotel in Masese, very close to the school. I stayed at the Panorama Hotel, overlooking Lake Victoria. Gorgeous view, not so good hotel. Well, what could I have expected if I was paying the equivalent of $18 per day with breakfast included? I was the only guest for most of the time. I got very friendly with the employees who were very nice but lacking essential training. For instance, if the power went off, I had to scream from my balcony "Gabriel, please turn on the generator" because he didn't think about it. Many times, he came back saying the hotel did not have oil to start the generator. Gabriel was like the manager and the cook, all in one, a very nice person indeed. His room was far away from my room, across the patio, so I had to scream at the top of my lungs from my balcony in the middle of the night. Hilarious!

During these two months, I worked non-stop with the sewing team. While they were sewing, I was taking the opportunity to make them realize how valuable they were. We discussed the role of the "man of the house," parenting in general, and family planning. I think if their men had listened to what I was sharing with their wives, I probably would have been shot. Especially, the day I gave them a payment for the pieces they had completed. I did it to entice them to continue with the project but clarified that from then on, they had to sell it in the local market.

Every afternoon, the owner of the Panorama Hotel allowed us to use space in the hotel garden to do our sewing work. She even gave us a space inside the hotel where we safely kept our stuff. Every afternoon, the women visited me at the hotel and spent the next four to five hours sewing. During the session I would offer them sodas and cookies, a real feast for them. Ugandans die for sodas!

All of them were so happy with the first payment they received, 40,000 UGX each

(US $12). They were discussing among themselves what to buy for the man of the house. I was so disappointed because I had seen that movie before. I suggested they keep the money hidden from the husbands/partners or use it immediately on their children and their school fees. Unfortunately, I was asking for too much! Their culture was more Important than my suggestions. The following week they said to me, "if I had listened to you Morella, I wouldn't have lost my entire earnings." Their "fabulous" men "took the money, bought alcohol, and left with another woman."

In the Ugandan culture, some women are under the dictatorship of the man of the house. Such women will do anything to keep their men. It gives them status to say they have a man, even if useless. There is no family planning. Women have eight to ten or more children. In the majority of the cases, if a woman or a man remarries and the new partner doesn't want the children from previous marriages, they are abandoned to their own luck or left in the hands of grandparents, who are already struggling to feed themselves.

For the most part, women in rural areas are brainwashed to think that they are second to men. They feel their job in life is to please men and have children. For many men, to say they have several children is a matter of pride, as it is a culture of "machos." I have also met many Ugandan men that are very good fathers; responsible and loving; who provide for and guide their children; who see their wives as their equal and not as their servants. Moses my driver, Ronny Sitanga

203

our treasurer, Pastor Frederick, and Pastor Paul Betambuze are examples of good husbands and fathers.

In this region, women dress covering the lower part of their bodies with long skirts. Showing their curves is considered too sexy. However, the upper part could be tight or loose showing part of their breast with no problem. During my first few trips, I followed their culture and wore long skirts. Thereafter, I decided to wear loose pants and long tops. I couldn't stand long skirts in a very hot weather, difficult to wear when climbing or walking across fields. In Kampala many more women wear pants or even short skirts and high heels but not in Jinja and Masese.

After that second trip, I visited Uganda many times, either with Jean Kaye or just by myself. I felt very safe walking around, going to church, or to the Jinja market with Moses, my driver, translator, and friend. I never had any incident or uncomfortable situations. Quite the opposite, I always felt very safe there.

In Uganda, "the whites" are called "Muzungus." I love it when the children cannot pronounce the word and call me something that sounds like "muchungo." For some children, seeing a white person is scary. One day I was attending mass in Walukuba and the woman in front of me was carrying her two to three years old baby boy. He was facing the altar but at one point he turned his face to me and started screaming as if he had seen a ghost! That was funny! In Kampala there are more whites but in this relatively small village many times I felt I was the only Muzungu.

Every Sunday, I attended mass at the church of the Annunciation in Walukuba. I befriended the priest and some parishioners. The priest asked me to teach two hours of catechism on Saturdays. So, I did. I really enjoyed talking and singing with the children and taking instant pictures of them. They loved to see their own pictures.

One day, the priest told me that the roof of the church was made of asbestos and there were no bathrooms for the assembly during the weekend masses. Initially, I thought that maybe the cost was going to be in the vicinity of $1000. Later, he said the proposals to fix it was in the vicinity of $23 thousand. I promised to think about it and get back to him. In reality, I knew I wasn't going to be able to find that amount of money.

One day I woke up in the middle of the night with the idea to contact Arturo Sosa SJ, the Superior General of the Society of Jesus. He reports to the Pope. It was a long shot but "hey, there is no harm trying!" I wrote him a letter asking for advice. I did not ask for the money directly, Humm! After waiting for about four months, I thought nothing was going to happen. Well, to my surprise, his office in Africa contacted me. Fortunately, I was in Jinja at that time and was able to visit the Regional Head of the Jesuits. He was based in Kenya but was visiting in Kampala at that time. I went there with Fr. Kibumya and Fr. Anthony from the church in Walukuba.

We left Jinja before 5 a.m. to avoid the torturous traffic to Kampala. We took with us the estimates and every piece of the document we thought was going to be necessary. The Regional priest was very gentle but firm. He didn't say yes. However, he was suggesting to Fr. Kibumya how to manage the project. He gave us the feeling our project was approved, although he told us that the response was going to be communicated to us in about three months. What??? The three longest months of our lives. Long story short, we got the full amount. I couldn't believe it! Now the only Catholic church in Masese had a new roof and a new bathroom. God is great and He takes care of His people!

It was in this church where I received a "Biblical" lesson. A very poor girl from the school, Titin Irene, used to meet me every Sunday at mass. She called me grandma because my son Eddie and his wife were her sponsors. One day, during mass, she was seated next to me and I noticed she had a small handkerchief in her hands. Different from other parts of the world, by the time of the offering, the baskets are in the front of the altar. I stood up and walked toward the altar to deposit my offering when I saw she was also coming behind me. I thought that she just wanted to be with me all the time. I opened my wallet and picked the paper money that I saw first, while she opened her small handkerchief and offered a coin. She was giving all she had, whereas I gave what I didn't need! Immediately, I remembered the humble widow passage in the Bible:

Luke 21:1-4

As Jesus looked up, he saw the rich putting their gifts into the temple treasury. ² He also saw a poor widow put in two very small copper coins.³ "Truly I tell you," he said, "this poor widow has put in more than all the others. ⁴ All these people gave their gifts out of their wealth but she out of her poverty put in all she had to live on."

I just experienced it. She did what the widow did. I am sure it was painful for her to offer all she had. Her coin was big-time more meaningful in the eyes of the Lord than what I gave. What a lesson!

St. Mother Theresa of Calcutta used to say, "give until it hurts, that the Lord will compensate you." I am sure Titin Irene gave all she had because I knew her story, I knew where she lived, and that coin represented all she had. She gave until it hurt her. What I have experienced in Uganda is that the less people have, the more generous they are.

They don't think about tomorrow, all they have is the present.

Uganda to me has been a world of lessons, an opportunity to grow my faith, to give love, and receive a hundred times more.

As I mentioned, during my first trips to Uganda I used HELP International Primary School as my center of operations. It was there that I met Bonny.

During my first trip, as I was getting settled, Bonny was helping me with the suitcases full of sewing materials, school supplies, donations, medicines, and rosaries. Everywhere I travel to remote locations, I bring 400-700 rosaries as I made a promise to our Blessed Mother Mary to expand the devotion of praying the rosary. When Bonny saw the rosaries, he jumped and asked me to give him one because, he said, he was

Catholic. This first encounter was the beginning of a friendship transformed into a mother and son relationship. Besides, he was wearing a Yankee t-shirt! my favorite baseball team. Imagine, Catholic, Yankee, and with a great heart. I was sold on him! He was 25 years old when I met him in 2016.

Bonny took us around town and helped us with everything we needed. He was sweet, soft-spoken, and very resourceful.

One day, Jen and I asked Bonny to show us where he was living. My friend Jenifer and I walked with him to the tiny place he called home, a few steps from the school. It was only one room, with no bathroom, no kitchen, no windows, no water, no mosquito nets, nothing other than a mattress on the floor, two chairs, a few pots and other kitchen utensils on the floor. He shared the room with two other young boys he rescued from the streets. He used to cook outside his one-room house, using charcoal. The house with no windows was a very dark place.

I was touched by the generosity of this young man. He rescued these boys and also helped some families to pay school fees for their children. He provided counseling for children at the school. Bonny was always happy; yet, his salary was the equivalent of $45 per month before deductions. His big heart gave until it hurt but our Lord compensated him big time!

Bonny's attitude confirmed that we don't have to be rich to share with others. We only need a big heart to share what we have with the less fortunate and wait for nothing in return. I couldn't forget what I saw in him. I decided to sponsor Bonny. I presented my idea of sponsoring him to Jean and Ronny and although he was not a student, they accepted my petition.

Bonny once asked me if it was ok with me if he called me "mom." His mother had abandoned him, and he had a distant relationship with her. Of course, I said, yes.

Time has passed and he is now supporting both his father and mother. Isn't it something? Of course, I said, yes.

During my second trip, I found out that one of the teachers was building an annex to his house. Ritah helped me negotiate the rental fee. Bonny and his two friends moved into the annex. Instead of just a room, they also had a sitting room with windows. I bought the trio three of everything: beds, mattresses, mosquito nets, towels, pillows, etc. However, they were still using public bathrooms, but at least they were much better than before.

I started motivating Bonny to continue his education and I was willing to support him. He seemed unenthused. After I made many attempts to obtain an answer from him, he finally told me that his high school papers were lost with no possibility finding them. A second reason he provided is that he was not willing to go back to school with a younger group of kids to pick up where he left off.

Ever since, Bonny has been part of my life. Today, he lives in our Transition Home in Jinja. He lives in an annex to our house within the same compound. He has a private bathroom, closet, sitting area, and everything his big heart deserves. He continues to work at the school. Besides, he is the purchasing officer of our Transition

Home. God compensated his generous heart, big time!

I always joke when I said that in Uganda everybody is a pastor. In reality, there are many who have built their own church. In the end, they are all Christians trying to spread the word of God.

They are charismatic and born-again Christians. Their services are usually ostentatious with louder music. Their songs are all about praising the Lord and chanting and clapping their hands and making loud sounds.

Jean is the major sponsor of a local pastor's organization of about 100 pastors in Jinja District and its neighborhood. It is led by Pastor Frederick Ojambo. He is very involved with the school activities. He and his wife Rosette have a beautiful family with six children. Many times, we have gone to their homes and shared a meal prepared by Rosette.

I also met Pastor Paul Betambuze, who built his church on the other side of town in the area called Masese 3. He also has a pre-K school for neighboring children. Every time I go to Uganda, I visit his school and bring school supplies and food for the children. It is an enjoyable moment to see the children singing songs to visitors. They love to hold my hands as their possession and keep other kids from getting closer to me. It is like a sign of ownership!

During one of my trips to Uganda in early 2018, I asked Pastor Frederick to show me the place where he had a refuge for children, also in Masese. Jean Kaye was with us. I was moved by what I saw, a basic two contiguous rooms with four bunk beds each; one room for boys and one for girls, 0 to 17 years old. Sometimes he had 36 children sharing beds rather than a maximum of 16. The place had no water or power, no bathrooms, and food cooked using charcoal outside the house on the floor. The place is surrounded by mud and dirt; the "school" was a small shack with broken benches inside a few flimsy walls. The beauty of it though was the love shown to take care of these children whose fate would have been different. They would have been on the streets if Frederick did not have the determination to save them.

When I was in front of that place, I asked myself, how can I go back to the US and forget this? How was I going to remove from my heart the desolation I saw there? How could I pretend I didn't experience the tough situation of the place?

Immediately, I felt again the burning sensation of His calling. This time was loud and clear, this time the Lord was not leaving me off the hook. I had no doubt this was what He wanted me to do. I decided to propose a deal to Him. I said "Lord, if you want me here for real, you would have to open doors for me. I don't have the experience, the knowledge, the funds, and the age to start off a home for children."

Then, I told Jean, who was next to me, "Jean, I think the Lord wants me here." Right there, the first door opened because Jean offered HELP International as the NGO under which I could operate in the US. I was determined to act and not let go of the opportunity to love Him by serving the most vulnerable of His people. Jean was the first door! I reckon I was determined but deeply scared to fail the Lord.

The following day, I met with Pastor Paul Betambuze, as someone very well versed in procuring the license to operate orphanage/children homes in Uganda. Also, he had the experience dealing with government agencies. We discussed the process, cost, timing, etc. and agreed to communicate when he had more information.

Two days later, I started my return home. On the plane, I was lucky to sit in a 4-seats row all by myself. I was very tired and decided to sleep like a queen for a few hours. What happened next was a big surprise to me. I placed my head on the pillow and immediately I sat down, grabbed my iPad, and started to write everything about the new organization: the name, which was very clear to be reserved for St. Joseph; the vision, mission, processes, etc. It was like the Holy Spirit was telling me what to write. I didn't recognize myself. The energy, the commitment, and desire to go ahead. I was determined to act. This time it was no more pretending I didn't hear Him, or that I was confused. This time His calling was clear, and I felt humble to be selected to act on His behalf. I felt my heart exploding from the gift He was placing in my hands. I didn't think about anything except His mission and the importance of being alert about His directives to operate. I was sure He heard me and agreed with my request for doors to be opened. I was yet to be surprised and humbled about the many more doors He was going to open for me; actually, for His mission rather.

Upon my arrival, Adriana Mendoza, my friend from college, called me to ask about the trip. When I explained to her what was happening, she said: "I'm in, I will work with you!" Adriana became an invaluable gift to St. Joseph. She and I had many brainstorming sessions. We did the research and wrote on many flipcharts our ideas and those of the experts. After several sessions, we concluded that our focus should not be on an orphanage, but should be on a transition home for abandoned, abused, or neglected children under six years old. This period of 0-6 years old, is a window of opportunity to impact their brain development. Adriana is very strategic in her approach to projects. Her prior experience working at the United Nations has been a big advantage to us. Using what I had recorded on my iPad, our research helped us to fine-tune some areas. Adriana was another open door!

The reason for a transition home and not an orphanage is because children are better when they grow up and develop as part of a family. Besides, we don't want them to be orphans for the rest of their lives. As a transition home, our goal is to save their lives, provide them with a safe living environment, healthcare, proper nutrition and early childhood stimulation. At the same time, we work with their blood relatives to assess the possibility of family reintegration. If this is not possible, we will follow Uganda government regulations to identify foster parents for the children. The final approval is with the Probation Officer. If none of the two options work out for a child, we then pursue other viable options such as Catholic orphanages for children six years and up.

Adriana and I discussed the need to have our own website. We decided to identify someone who could help us as neither of us was a pro in that area. When she left, I started doing more research about websites. To my additional surprise, I designed the website myself! Yes, I did it myself using a friendly platform, but I did it. I called Andreina, my nice, who is a Graphic Designer and she designed our Logo, which represents the hands of St. Joseph protecting the children. Andreina was amazing and she did not want to charge me for the logo. Andreina was another open door!

In a matter of a few weeks, we had our website and logo ready. Adriana and I couldn't believe how far we had gone in just few weeks. By April 1, 2018 we were able to start off our first fundraising campaign. Our campaign was based on a vision because we did not have the transition home license yet, nor did we have the house or the staff. Yet, people donated funds to support God's project. Those who donated trusted our vision. I will forever be thankful for their generosity and trust.

One Saturday morning, I was in adoration at a small chapel next to the Parish I go to, St Mary Magdalen in Sunny Isle Beach, Florida. I was alone with the Lord telling Him what we had done. I was also asking Him how to do His Will with no funds and no volunteers in Uganda. He spoke to me saying that funds and volunteers were His problems and not mine. I thought my imagination had created His response in my mind. Well, that very next day, a friend of mine called me and asked me questions about the project. She gave me a check for ten thousand dollars! Yes, Ten Thousand dollars! The following day, a strange woman I never met before called me from Canada saying that she wanted to volunteer in Uganda. Two days following my encounter with the Lord! It was clear it was not my imagination but His real message. What a way to show me His plan! Another huge door opened!

It was at that very moment when I understood that the Uganda project was clearly His mission and not mine. He really wanted me to be the executor of His plan. How could I say no? How could I have pretended I didn't hear His voice if He was opening door after door? He delivered His part of the deal, now it was my turn to deliver mine! I felt blessed to have this opportunity to serve Him. He opened my eyes big time. This mission has made me humble by His grandiose love and mercy. I realized how and why He has been preparing me from my childhood to do His Will. In retrospect, I could see that my life, as the lives of all His children, are part of His plan. How we respond to His plan is up to each one of us. This is why it is very critical that we open our hearts and let the Holy Spirit transform us. We should open our eyes, our ears, our hearts to listen to His voice. This is the hardest thing to do, at least this had been my experience. Many times before, I either was not listening, distracted or I was scared to acknowledge His calling. Nevertheless, His time is perfect and perhaps this was the best time for me to do His Will.

The beginning of our organization was very rocky. I went back to Uganda in July,2018 to formally apply for the license and search for a place for our transition home. I visited the Probation Officer in charge of the approval process. Point-blank he told me that he was not going to grant me the license. I became frustrated and I turned to Jean Kaye. Coincidentally she was also in Masese at that time. I told her that if I didn't have the license, I didn't have the project. I was going back to the US. Jean, who is a very wise Christian, said to me "Morella when the Lord asked you to do this, He never told you it was going to be easy. So, find the way."

I internally reviewed my agreement with the Lord, realizing one more time that this project was His project. He was going to open more doors for me. I went ahead, took a leap of faith, and searched for the house. Many people thought I was insane to incur the transition home expenses before I had secured the license yet. After reflecting on the past few months and my conversation with Jean, I knew He was in control.

Through my friend Solomon Kabuka, I got in contact with the Rotary Clubs in Jinja and Mukono. As a matter of fact, they invited me as a speaker to present our plan. He and I prepared the first three phrases in Luganda, one of the local languages. It was very hard to deliver. Luganda pronunciation is very difficult for us, Muzungus. It started like this:

Nsimye nyo, okufuna omukisa okubera

namwe okwogera ku project St. Joseph's Shining Little Stars. Meaning: I am very pleased for this opportunity to be with you and talk about the project SJSLS. I memorized the entire piece after repeating it over and over again. It made a big impact on the audience. The Rotarians were very receptive about the project. One of the Rotarians helped me find the house in Jinja. I went on and signed a one-year contract and furnished the house.

It was funny that before I went to Uganda, my dear friend Alicia Carrazana told me that I was going to find the house on July 27, and sure enough I found it on July 27th, 2018.

In Uganda, to apply for the license, the house must be furnished, with staff already trained. It took me several conversations with the Probation Officer. Unfortunately, he needed some "appreciation money" upfront before I could be granted the license to operate. Government agencies are very corrupted, but I got it. The Lord showed me the way!

Sometimes the Lord sends His messengers through a friend and in this case, Jean was His messenger. Doing His Will is challenging and even scaring, that is why He asks us to walk by faith and not by sight!

Early in the process, Pastor Paul Betambuze was going to Kampala to register our organization. He asked me for the name of the organization and I said, "St. Joseph's Shining Little Stars". He asked me for option two, in case the name has already been taken. I said, "there is no second option. I guarantee you this is the name." This name was not my creation. It came to me in the plane, on my way back to the USA when I was inspired by the Holly Spirit about the vision and mission of the project. Pastor Paul was annoyed by my answer and insisted in having a second option. My answer was the same, there is no option 2. Sure enough, the name had not been taken!

As soon as I came back, I was communicating to Father Kirlin everything that happened to me in Uganda. He looked at me and said that since I was from the parish, he was going to sponsor our project. Every December during one full weekend the second collection during each one of the four masses was dedicated to our foundation. He allowed me to present a video and to speak to the assembly. This was a huge door the Lord opened for us. Every year for two consecutive years, we collected almost one third of our entire budget! Father Kirlin retired and I was afraid the new priest, Father Damian, would not continue with the parish support. Thank God, Father Damian decided to continue sponsoring us.

Finally, in early February 2019, we obtained the license, and a few weeks after, our first child, Kauthara, arrived.

Kauthara's mother died at birth. Her father had five other children to take care for. He had to give his moto-taxi as a collateral to get a loan to bury his wife. We took Kauthara with us and thanks to two donors, we paid off his father's loan. He was able to get his moto-taxi back and continue caring for the other five children.

Every child has a sad story behind. We are there to protect them and help them develop into healthy and prosperous human beings.

One day, one of our donors said that we needed a playground. I said I agreed but we had other priorities. Long story short, she gave us the money to buy and install it in our garden with the request to call it "the Garden of St. Anne", the mother of our Blessed Mother Mary.

I asked Moses to take me to different places to search for playgrounds. We visited several places, but he always asked me to stay in the car. When store owners see a Muzungu, prices double or triple! A few months later, the playground was installed in the garden of St Anne.

At the moment I am writing this book, we have eight children living in our transition home. In total, we have been able to support more than 50 children. Some through orphanages in the region. In other cases, we have supported blood relatives who have kept their children and continued to care for them. One of these later cases was Emmanuel. His mother was a 17 years old girl with a breast tumor. Her partner abandoned her (or so she said) and with no money to purchase baby formula Emmanuel was getting malnourished. We bought baby formula, pampers and gave her some clothes for him. In addition, we bought his mom's medicines and enrolled her in tailoring classes at Help School. Eventually, his mother will earn a living to support her son, and Emmanuel will stay with his own family.

Each time I return to Uganda, the children in our house, except for Kauthara, spend the first day or two somehow scared of me.

Thereafter, they are stamped to my body, holding to me as if I am going to escape. Kauthara is different, at her first sight of me, she comes to me directly. We both have a special bond. I wish I were 20 years younger to adopt her and bring her with me to the USA. I don't want to think about the day she will return to her family. At the end, this is one of the challenges of loving these children as if they were our owns.

Our organization is getting in better shape now. I am confident we will grow as much as the Lord wants us to grow. We now have three caregivers living at home with the children; plus, security guards, a manager, and a poultry/garden worker. Coincidentally, all of them are Catholic and I assure you I never asked for their faith before I hired them.

The compound is very large. I decided to purchase 100 chickens and plant 12 types of vegetables to secure a healthy diet for our children. We could sell the excess in the local market and use the funds to cover some house expenses. I asked Moses, my driver if he knew someone in the market who I could hire for the poultry and garden. He brought Geoffrey, an exceptional and a very committed worker.

We extended the room at the extreme south of the compound and prepared it to receive the 100 chicks. They arrived on a Thursday evening. Geoffrey placed containers with charcoal and special lights to warm the place all day long. On Friday morning, I woke up very early and run outside to see the new guests. To my surprise I found Geoffrey sleeping on the floor next to the chicks. He said he felt this project was his project, and he needed to protect his chicks from dying. Wow!

I learned about laying chickens and their time to lay eggs, which is only 16 months. After this period, they would be sold as meat and new ones will replace them. For the first 16 months, our poultry produced 80 eggs per day. We sold the surplus in the market and the proceeds helped us to pay for some expenses.

Geoffrey also prepared the land for planting 12 types of vegetables. Some of those, were totally new to me, such as "dodo" and "sukumawiki." Both green vegetables are high in protein and taste very nice indeed.

In the compound, there is an additional structure with two bedrooms. One for my

Ugandan son, Bonny, and the other for the security guard and the poultry worker.

I am very pleased to have Bonny living with us. Once a week, he gets the list of food and home articles needed. He goes to the market and purchases them for us.

We also have a local board of directors composed of Ronny Sitanga as treasurer, Pastor Paul Betambuze as the board secretary, Father Paul from the parish of Our Lady of Fatima, and Moses, as directors.

In the meantime, back in the US, Adriana and I run the foundation. She takes care of the office administration activities. I look for funds and program administration matters.

I have been blessed to have volunteers traveling with me. Specially, Yudelka Solano, MD. She is a tireless supported of the mission and the community. She travels with suitcases full of medicines and donations. She sees patients and treat them with love and respect. We also enjoy going to Jinja main street searching for art craft.

One of the reasons why I worked my entire life was because I didn't like to ask for money to cover my personal expenses. I never thought I was going to be effective asking for contributions. My joke is that I have become an international beggar. I am no longer shy or so people think. The reality is that asking for money is not something that comes easy for me; but with practice, I have become a bit better. The fact is that through three campaigns, we have collected more than $100,000.

In addition, every time I go to Uganda, I purchase art craft and jewelry made from recycled paper and I sell it in the US for substantially more. The proceeds are returned to Uganda to support the transition home.

I have met many good people in Uganda, one of them is Moses. He is my driver but as I said before, he is also my interpreter and my friend. He has a wife, Olivia, and three children. He is a good father, husband, and a great human being.

When I am in Uganda, I love to go with him to the Jinja Central Market. In some way, it is an organized disaster. Produces are fresh and delicious. Outside, on the street walk, trash is everywhere, and it is hardly removed. Inside, vendors leave their debris on the floor and no one bothers to pick it up. My favorites fruits are sweet bananas, mangoes, and pineapples.

The streets in Jinja are half with concrete and half just dirt and mud. There are thousands of boda-boda (moto-taxis), no traffic lights, and no one obeying basic rules. Pedestrians are left out of luck, praying for their lives when crossing the streets.

Jinja's main street is full of art craft shops and some small restaurants with local food. My favorite place is called Igar's Café, which offers great pizzas and vegetable curry. Usually, I only have two meals a day. I have breakfast at home and around four pm, if I am running errands, I go with Moses to Igar's or Sergiou's, also for pizza. These are the only type of food I eat while I am there, pizza or vegetable curry. I like fish but they serve it with the head and the tail, and I rather die than see the eyes of the fish.

Sometimes on Sundays, I cook at home for the staff and Bony. We like to eat outside under the huge mango tree we have in the back of the house, next to the playground. The staff look forward to this special treat. Every time I am in Uganda, I host a special party for the children, their siblings if any, and a close relative. It is important to establish a strong bond between the children and their families.

I enjoy very much walking every day to the church, which is around two blocks from our house. I meet the nuns from the convent close to our house, and we walk together. Sometimes the cows of our neighbors also walk with us!

I usually travel to Uganda at least three times per year. I wish I could do it more frequently. Unfortunately, being the principal fundraiser, my main goal is to ensure that the budget is secured to support our mission, and our donors are away from this side of the world.

What will happen to me next? What will The Lord ask me to do next? I don't know. I only know that today He wants me focused on this project. Tomorrow? He only knows, but I am ready for when He decides. I now know I didn't have the knowledge, experience, funds, and the age to start off this mission but He had, so He did!

Solomon

A s I mentioned earlier, every time I travel to Africa, I bring with me 500 or more rosaries. They are made by the "Rosary Makers of Weston", a group of volunteers that make rosaries all year long. My friend Alexandra is my link to this group. One day, she asked me to visit these ladies because they wanted to know more about where their rosaries had traveled to. Finally, I was able to visit them on a Monday morning. I took with me some jewelry gifts from Uganda as appreciation for what they have done.

I was fascinated to visit the group of about twenty-five women enjoying their time together, helping each other while making rosaries. They wanted to know everything about the project, so I told them the story in detail since the beginning of my journey. As I was standing in front of them, I recognized a woman who had gone to school with my sister Pachy back in Venezuela some 50 years ago. I tried to make eye contact with her, but she didn't respond, which made me doubt if she was who I thought she was.

When I finally approached her, she said she knew me as well as my face resembled my sister Pachy's face. This is funny because everybody says the same, that all of us look very much alike. I guess an apple never falls far from the tree! We started chatting and she said I should contact her former neighbor, Dr. Solomon Kabuka, because he was from Uganda, had lived in the USA for over forty years, and he also had a humanitarian foundation. She thought he could help me. She gave me his contact information. I took the piece of paper, put it in my purse, and completely forgot about it. It was days later when I remembered the incident and decided to call him, after I consulted with Google, of course!

The first time I called him, he said he was on the other line with Uganda and that he was going to call me back. A few days later, after when he didn't call, I decided to send him a text message. He said he has been busy but, in the meantime, he sent me his own foundation's website for me to review it. I did it quickly and decided to send him a text saying that I now was more interested in talking to him because I thought "there may be a reason why our paths were crossing." Every time I think about this comment I laugh because I have never been so pushy.

Eventually, he called me back and offered to meet me for half-hour, the day before his trip to Ireland.

That day was a Thursday, when I usually serve as a volunteer in the house of the Malta Knights-Cuba chapter in West Flagler, one hour away from Weston where the meeting with Solomon was to take place.

I arrived right on time after a horrible traffic jam at 1 pm. He greeted me with some joke at the lobby and we went straight to the restaurant located on the grounds of his condo. After our introductions, we sat down and started a very interesting conversation. He asked me about my foundation, and he told me about his experiences with his foundation. Rather than a half-hour, we talked non-stop for three hours. We shared the same passion for serving others. We talked about so many topics, including his desire to visit the Maracaibo Lake and Angel's Falls in Venezuela. I offered to go with him as his tour guide. I said to myself, 'I will do anything as long as he supports our Uganda project!' I really enjoyed the conversation and was fascinated by his personality but nothing else. We said goodbye and I wished him a good trip the day after.

As I was driving back to my house, I received a WhatsApp from him asking for my picture because, according to him, he travels to many places and takes pictures of the people he meets to remember them. He sent me his, but I said to myself, 'I am not going to send this man a picture of me!' but at the same time, I said, 'well if I don't, he probably will not help my foundation.' I decided to send him the same picture that was on my website available to the public. I wanted his support but not a personal involvement.

The following day, he sent me one of those online videos wishing me a good day. I said to myself, 'oh I hope this guy is not going to be one of those high maintenance guys who will bombard me with videos and pictures.' I thanked him and told him I was visiting a radio station for an interview regarding Mater Filius. A few hours later he was asking about the interview.

Later he sent me another picture at the airport and then another one when he arrived in Ireland and on and on the entire week. We were connected the entire week. We spoke or chatted for hours and hours. Now that I know him well, I realize he is a fanatic picture-taker and enjoys keeping contact with everybody he meets.

During the entire time he was in Ireland I was imploring the Lord to remove him from my life. I was very happy with my life and I didn't need any complications. When people used to say to me that I was lonely I replied, "not at all, I live alone but I am not lonely."

My life was completed between my volunteering work, my children, my family, my parish, and my friends, and moreover, with my love for the Lord. I was afraid Solomon might bring a detour to the plan I have designed for the rest of my days. Every day my plead to the Lord was the same, 'please Lord take him away from my path.' I was so afraid of him that I even asked Adriana my friend to go out with him instead of me. I was afraid of moving away from the plan I have designed for myself.

When he came back to the USA, he visited me several times and our chats continued. Long story short, we have been together for over two years. I remember going to Father Kirlin concerned because Solomon and this new relationship was not part of my plan. Father Kirlin reminded me that God's plan was not a copycat of my plan and that I just needed to pray and ask the Lord for guidance.

From the book of Isaiah (55:8-9):

For my thoughts are not your thoughts
nor your ways are my ways, says the Lord
For as the heavens are higher than the
earth,
So are my ways higher than your ways,
and my thoughts higher than your thoughts.

I wasn't looking to have a new person in my life, as opposed to Solomon, who was actively looking for a partner. Our love for each other has grown day by day. We have fun together, playing bowling, cooking, traveling, praying, and even laughing about our own limitations, which at our age are many. We always say we are two disabled people helping each other. Solomon is four years older than me, even though he looks much younger than his age. We are very different and yet, we are very similar. We want to make the other person happy and we are willing to go the extra mile to bring happiness to our relationship.

Solomon has reduced my hyper-personality at least two levels! I now enjoy simple things I didn't enjoy before. I was always looking to do something outside of my home because staying at home for me before I met him was like time wasted. I now enjoy having a good conversation with him or even cooking together or just enjoying a sunset.

Solomon was raised as Anglican. Since we started dating, he has accompanied me to Sunday's church. I value it very much because he knows how important going to church to celebrate my faith is for me. There are many areas of Christianity where he and I have different opinions. He challenges many aspects written in the Bible while to me everything that is written there is true.

Falling in love at this age has been a blessing! I didn't realize how "cool" is to have a friend with whom to share our lives. Saying and doing the things we did when falling in love during our early twenties is amazing. Age should not be a limitation to enjoy happiness. I remember how my parents enjoyed their love even in their late 80's.

As soon as I started dating Solomon, I flew to NYC to see my sons. I wanted them to know it directly from me. From there, I first called my oldest son who lives in Caracas. He said this was my life and I was free to do whatever I wanted. He thanked me for letting him know it in advance.

Immediately after, I had lunch with Eddie in Bryan Park in NYC. Once I told him about Solomon, his first reaction was a genuine expression of happiness. He was extremely happy for me. He supported me big time. Eddie is very open-minded, and his explanation was: "mom if you are happy, I am happy, actually very happy you are not alone."

I saved the most difficult for last. Eddy with a "Y" wasn't a happy camper. It has been difficult for Eddy to accept my relationship with Solomon and the fact that I am not only his mom but a woman at my age in love. I understand how he feels. He has gotten a bit better but still, a bit reserved when I mention anything about Solomon.

Patty, his wife, has been great. She has supported me as a daughter would have done it. Very warm and attentive when we talk about Solomon. I know she has "massaged" Eddy's brain a lot. One day, Eddy said to me that if I was happy, he was ok.

My sisters and immediate friends have been a different story. They all have been very supportive of my relationship with Solomon. They have met him, and including my nieces and nephews, they all like him and are very happy for me.

In 2019, when one of my nephews was getting married in Madrid, Solomon decided to change his plans from attending a Rotary International Conference in Germany and travelled with me to attend the wedding. We spent three weeks in total to tour Spain and France. We travelled by train from Madrid to Barcelona. Later, we drove from Barcelona to France to visit Our Lady of Lourdes. From there we drove through the Alps mountains, overnighted in Zaragoza and took a train back to Madrid. It was a great trip and an opportunity to meet more members of my big family.

One day, back in Florida, while Solomon was driving, I was on the phone with Kico, my sister, who was in Chile with Parkinson's disease. I was a bit emotional and when I finished the conversation, he asked me if I wanted to go and visit my sister in Chile. I was surprised because we were supposed to celebrate Solomon's birthday with his family in Los Angeles. He said, "if Kico is important to you, then she is important to me too." I couldn't be happier. This action from his part made him win big points.

We went to Chile and spent more time with the family than we ever thought; the night before we arrived in Santiago, the capital, riots and political unrest started. So, we couldn't leave the house. My nieces developed a strong bond with Solomon to the point that I sometimes know more about my Chilean family through him than directly from them.

Solomon has a great heart and is very perceptive to the needs of the poor. Through his SK Global Empowering Network Foundation, he supports very needy people in Uganda, India, Haiti and other Caribbean islands. He has a mentoring program to develop young leaders across these countries, counsel those starting their new business ventures to ensure success and improve their quality of life. As a retired professor of International Business and Management, he now teaches classes ad honorem to support a raising crop of leaders in Haiti.

Solomon has been a key supporter of my Uganda foundation. His suggestions and connections both in the US and locally in

Uganda have helped us advance our mission. He is a great sounding board! It was through his contacts in Jinja that we found the house for our project. Also, through his local contacts I was given time at the Rotary Clubs in Mukono and in Jinja to present our foundation and increase our presence there.

This is the type of person that God has brought to my life. He has become my best friend. We share our thoughts, anxiety, concerns, happiness, pictures of our family and friends, jokes, everything. We are committed to each other, to our wellbeing, and our happiness.

In terms of our future together one thing is for sure, we want to be there for each other and enjoy each other's company, while we also help those in need. We always laugh when we compare how each other has spent the day. We frequently say that we are retired. However, we dedicate much of our days helping and solving people's problems.

I have learned to enjoy the day, each day at a time, and give thanks to the Lord for, among other blessings, introducing Solomon to my life.

Understanding my journey

According to St. Paul (1 Cor, 12:4-25), Faith is a spiritual gift of God. "It is Him who in His infinite love and mercy, does marvelous things in our hearts and minds. It is through Him that our faith grows when we surrender our wills to the Will of God. It is the absolute trust and confidence in the Lord's plan and ways, even beyond human comprehension. This spiritual gift of Faith is not for personal enrichment but instead, for building up others within the church."

Faith is a gift of God, comparable to a beautiful plant that must be watered constantly or will dry out and eventually die. To me, faith and love are always together. My love for the Lord increases my faith and vice-versa. Love is the water that makes my plant grows. However, I cannot love someone I don't know.

There has been in my life people that have been examples of how to water my Faith and fall in love with the Lord. One of these people is Teresita Sulbaran, my adopted sister. Teresita is the "total package" when it comes to defining Faith in the Lord, and love to the neighbors. She is very spiritual and savvy. Many times, priests and medical doctors have sent her people who needed spiritual guidance or people who were dealing with serious illness. She encourages them to drop off their needs in His hands. When I call her for advice, just by listening to her voice and suggestions, I feel at peace. She definitely, has been a source of inspiration to me.

Teresita had a card with the image of the Virgin Mary in her advocation of the Virgin of Perpetual Help in one of her tables in her living room. One day, she realized the little card was very oily, so she cleaned it. The following day she saw the table oily again, so she cleaned it one more time until she saw that the oil was coming from inside the little card. Every day, the card was dropping oil. I have seen it with my own eyes, otherwise I think I would've doubted it. Many people go to her house and take cotton balls with drops of oil to people who are suffering from any illness. Once a month Teresita hosts a prayer and more than of one hundred people go there to pray and to hear living testimonies from those who claimed to be cured after they received the oil from the Virgin of Perpetual Help's little card.

Teresita is a very special person in my life and actually in the lives of my entire family. My parents loved her very much and I know they treated her as their daughter number 9.

When I retired in 2015, I decided to enroll as a volunteer in different non-profits organizations around the Miami area. I felt a connection to some more than to others. One of the organizations I worked with was Respect Life, which provides counseling to pregnant low-income women. It also provides them essentials for the newborns for one full year after birth. One day, Maggie, the head of the office, gave me a book, "The 33 Days Consecration to Virgin Mary." It was a meditation with our Blessed Mother Mary. This book changed my life! It was a direct conversation with Mary and her recommendations about how to fall in love with Her Son. Reading the book, I learned that in order to fall in love with Him, it is imperative to get to know Him closely; and the best way was by reading the Bible and understanding His message, receiving Communion, attending daily mass, taking care of the most needed, praying the rosary and meditating, as a direct conversation with the Lord.

I used to go to mass only on Sundays and special days of observation. I read portions of the Bible at a maximum speed limit and seldom prayed the rosary; a reading pace that did not leave much room for comprehension. After consecrating my life to our Blessed Mother Mary, I started reading the Bible in a disciplined way, enjoying the passages, and trying to understand His message and its application to my daily life.

Praying the rosary is an intimate conversation with our Blessed Mother as we remember every phase in the life of Jesus. I pray the rosary every day and feel a closer connection to Jesus and mother Mary. Praying the rosary has become part of my daily routine. Sometimes, I wake up at night and realize I have been praying the rosary in my mind. Prayers make me feel stronger and better prepared for the challenges I face.

St. Mother Theresa of Calcutta said:
"I used to believe that prayer changes things, but now I know that prayer changes us, and we change things."

Attending daily Mass and receiving Communion are the opportunities to have an intimate relationship with Him. Communion gives me peace and fills up my heart with His immense love.

I am still learning how to listen to His voice rather than the monologue I used to have after Communion. I now try to stay silent, in adoration, attentive to His voice. Sometimes He says something, sometimes we just see each other's eyes with love. I feel His arms around me, protecting me. I feel His love and His mercy.

When I receive His peace and feel His immense love, it is very easy for me to give to others. My heart explodes if I kept them just for me. Behavior and actions toward others become natural. I feel compelled to give and share love to others regardless of who they are, not because they are Christians but because I am.

There are people we like and people we dislike one way or another. What I am trying to do is to see Jesus's eyes in every person. This practice has made a significant change in the behavior I display to others. It is very difficult, but I keep trying.

I grew up as Catholic, went to a Catholic school, and a Catholic college. While I was growing up, almost everybody in Caracas was Catholic. Religion was not an issue when meeting new friends because, for the most part, our immediate surrounding friends were also Catholics. I venture to say that at the time I was growing up, 90% of the population of Venezuela was Catholic, 5% other Christian denominations, and 5% Jews.

My parents instilled in me the love for our Lord Jesus, and the respect for our neighbors. I learned the values and principles by experiencing them at home.

Different from my mom, my dad was not a religious person. He didn't go to church other than to attend weddings, Baptisms, or Holy Communion of any of his descendants. He believed in Jesus and demonstrated his beliefs during his entire life by supporting and loving those in need, but he was not a practicing Catholic. After his passing, we found that he had written some notes in preparation for a book he wanted to leave to his descendants. In the notes, he expressed his love for my mom and his eight girls and said, "they are the best capital God has given me." He also described his hobbies, first as hunting and fishing, later flying planes and golfing. As a hunter, he recalled killing many animals including deer and tigers, and ended up saying "why did I kill them? I only ask the Lord to forgive me because I think I was a criminal".

He had Faith but he was not religious at all, and actually, he was very critical of the priests in general. Few days before his death, he received the absolution from Cardenal Porras. He gave him the Holy Communion days before his passing.

My mom, on the other hand, had a strong faith and took us to church on Sundays at the Chiquinquira's Church, the parish we belonged to when we were very young. She made sure we were enrolled in a Catholic school and were sensitive to the needs of others less fortunate than us. She was devoted to the Virgin Mary in her advocation of the Virgin of Coromoto, patron of Venezuela and her favorite phrase was "if God allowed us…" Every night, she sat on the edge of her bed and prayed the rosary.

My first marriage was celebrated in a Catholic Church. I always thought my marriage was going to last forever and ever. Unfortunately, the problems started almost immediately. His personality asphyxiated me, and I didn't have the maturity to stop it until at one point it was impossible to continue. The marriage lasted a bit less than four years. I struggled in my marriage since day one and wanted to end the marriage during the first year. However, when I got married, I thought I married till death, so it was very difficult to end the marriage. In addition, that year my parents were having their 40th anniversary and I didn't want to upset them by having a divorce.

Even though they were not having a big celebration, I thought my divorce would ruin their year. It could also be considered an excuse for my lack of courage to end the marriage sooner. It was not easy to go through a divorce when in my entire family, including cousins, I was the first one to end a marriage.

One day, I questioned myself about the type of role model I wanted for my son and the type of life I was going to have when I was only 25 years old. It was very difficult for me to decide to divorce because of my Catholic upbringing. I convinced myself that the Lord didn't want me to stay in a toxic marriage.

When I made the decision, I visited Orlando, my brother in law, who was a lawyer with his own practice. He forwarded my case to one of his lawyers as he thought my parents were going to be upset if he did it himself.

Even though I was the one who wanted the divorce, the stress of feeling I was transgressing my beliefs was unbearable. I remember holding back my tears at work to avoid sharing my story with my co-workers. The marriage did not end well.

I didn't tell anyone about my decision to go ahead with the separation until after we had gone in front of the judge to sign the papers. I went to my parents afterward and explained, to their surprise, what I had done. After my mother crying non-stop and my dad's full support of my decision, they understood I was not coming back home but staying with my son in my rental apartment. At that time, a divorced woman living alone with her child was not well perceived, but I did it anyway.

The reason I didn't tell anyone about my decision to go ahead with the separation was because I didn't want to be influenced one way or the other. This was perhaps the most important decision in my life so far and I wanted it to be mine. At that time, to end a marriage was a two-year separation first and then the divorce was granted. There was no way to accelerate it.

I married my second husband in a civil wedding and stopped having Communion until I had a discussion with a priest in the parish where I lived, El Placer in Caracas. I narrated to the priest what my first marriage had been, and he encouraged me to ask the church for the annulment. At that time, it was a very difficult process and only reserved for people with contacts in the Vatican or so we thought.

I remember the case of Caroline of Monaco, who got her annulment in a heartbeat and the press highlighting the contacts they had in the Vatican. Maybe it was true or not, but the effect of this annulment had on many people was not good.

I told the priest that I thought the annulment was going to harm my son if, eventually, I said to him that the marriage with his father never existed.

After several hours with the priest, he misguided me and gave me the permission to take Communion again and asked me not to confess it ever again. To me, it was the best gift I ever received. There is another way to receive Jesus in our heart, the Spiritual Communion, but it is not comparable to directly receiving the body and blood of our Lord Jesus Christ. I recently found out that the priest should not have given me the permission because he was not authorized to do it. I should have followed the lengthy process including the final approval from the Vatican. Later the process changed so that the final approval is in the hands of the Archbishop. As a matter of fact, if either the wife or the husband requests the annulment and presents all the necessary documentation and the other person either is not in agreement or cannot be localized, the process continues. When the final approval is made, they are notified.

In the Bible, Jesus's message is all based on love and forgiveness. I grew up with a sense of guilt, everything was a sin, and God was there to judge and to keep a list of all our transgressions throughout our lives. The big difference is that repentance, forgiveness, and His immense mercy erase our faults. Our Lord is a loving God, who knows about our weaknesses and sees us with His fatherly eyes. He is not the God who punishes but the God who understands our flaws and sees our resolution to not repeat them.

As I grew older, I started to understand that what matters is my relationship with the Lord. It has not been an easy development and it has taken several years, dialogues with priests and friends. I was more concerned about religion than about my intimate relationship with the Lord. I am convinced

He sees our intentions, knows our past and our particular situations. He is a God of immense love for us, who wants our wellbeing and more importantly, who has a place for us in heaven.

Matthew 25:33-34

He will put the righteous people at His right and the others at His left.

Then the King will say to the people on his right "Come, you that are blessed by my Father! Come and possess the kingdom which has been prepared for you ever since the creation of the world.

Early on in my life, repentance was all about sins I had committed according to the teaching of the Church. Now, repentance is about the feeling of having hurt Jesus directly.

I used to take the Holy Communion and be the one talking in a monologue, always asking Him for something. I wasn't aware that if I was the one talking, I didn't allow Him to interrupt me. I am now learning to listen and stay quiet to hear His voice, which is not easy, it takes practice. Sometimes I found myself going back to the monologue mode.

I was writing this book and realized how every moment, every experience I had in life was all concatenated. Sometimes difficult to see it as I was going through life but in retrospect, there was a reason for every moment, for every experience I lived.

What has been the single most significant aspect of my life? Obviously, there are many. The birth of my children and grandchildren, and my life with my parents; all these are monumental. However, from the perspective of my faith there is one which marked my life big time. It was the moment when I was in adoration and the Lord told me He was going to take care of the funding and volunteers for the St Joseph project in Uganda. Why? Because I was asking His help for "my" mission. When during the next two days I received a check for ten thousand dollars, and the call from a lady in Canada offering to go with me to Uganda as a volunteer, I realized first it was true He said what I heard Him saying. Second, I understood the Uganda project was His mission and not my mission.

Even this year, as we live through this horrible pandemic that has taken so many lives, I have not been able to host fundraising events, but the project's checking account has not decreased. The Lord takes care of it.

He picked me to work for Him, knowing that I had no experience or knowledge, but He knew that nothing was impossible for Him. There is a famous phrase that says that the Lord doesn't choose the qualified but enables the selected. He did His everything!

I feel the privilege to work for Him, to be able to serve others on His behalf; even to ask for money, which I don't enjoy, or to travel to Uganda 36 hours door-to-door. In Uganda, if our work can impact the life of only one of those children, I will consider my effort fully paid.

I am blessed to live the life I have had so far, even with my ups and downs, with my own failures and successes. I look forward with optimism to whatever His plan has for me. Amen.

About the author:

Morella grew up in Venezuela as one of eight sisters. After finishing her bachelor's degree in Caracas, she completed her M.S. in Human Development from Pace University, Lubin School of Business, New York City.

She worked for forty years in Human Resources in Global Corporations in the banking and technology industries.

She retired in 2015 to dedicate her life to serving others.

Her volunteering career took off first in Peru in Latin America, and later in Malawi and Uganda in Africa. In February 2018 she committed herself to start up a transition home for abused, abandoned, or neglected children under six years old in Jinja, Uganda; at that moment, St. Joseph's Shining Little Stars was born.

Morella now has three sons and three grandchildren and lives in Florida.

Through the Eyes of My Soul, by Morella
Echenagucia-Carta, was printed in USA,

October 2020